Many years ago I asked A̲ so many women in these End Times. His answer was: Because they are better House Cleaners and I want My House cleaned up!

Jasmine is a great House Cleaner. It is urgent to cleanse His House from all stereotypes and discrimination concerning women. Another time the Spirit whispered to me the word "abortions". He told me that He puts His visions and dreams inside of His Women. When they do not answer the Call because of fear or religious discrimination, it is His "babies" that are being aborted. This powerful book will help women to never abort their callings. You will know the Truth, and the Truth as brought forth by Jasmine with great skill, anointing and knowledge will make you free to be all you were created to be!

In Yeshua's Amazing Love,

—Bishop Dr. Dominiquae Bierman
Minister, Author and Psalmist
Eilat, Israel
www.kad-esh.org

"For Zion's sake I will not keep silent".

—Isaiah 62:1

Sullied BRIDE

JASMINE ANDREWS

CREATION
HOUSE

Sullied Bride by Jasmine Deanne Andrews
Published by Creation House
A Charisma Media Company
600 Rinehart Road
Lake Mary, Florida 32746
www.charismamedia.com

Unless otherwise noted, quotations from the Quran are from *The Qur'an: Text, Translation and Commentary* by Abdullah Yusuf Ali, published by Tahrike Tarsile Quran, Inc., P.O. Box 1115, Corona-Elmhurst Station, Elmhurst, New York 11373-1115, US Edition 1987.

All Hebrew definitions are taken from Dr. Reuven Sivan and Dr. Edward A. Levenston, *The New Bantoam-Megiddo Hebrew and English Dictionary* (New York: Bantam Books, 2009); Gary D. Pratico and Miles V. Van Pelt, *Basic of Biblical Hebrew Grammar 2nd ed.* (Grand Rapids, MI: Zondervan, 2007).

Design Director: Justin Evans
Cover design by Lisa McClure

Library of Congress Control Number: 2015913997
International Standard Book Number: 978-1-62998-494-0
E-book International Standard Book Number:
978-1-62998-495-7

While the author has made every effort to provide accurate telephone numbers and Internet addresses at the time of publication, neither the publisher nor the author assumes any responsibility for errors or for changes that occur after publication.

First edition

16 17 18 19 20 — 987654321
Printed in the United States of America

CONTENTS

HOW DID THIS HAPPEN?

*A*LL OVER THE world women are oppressed and treated as second-class citizens. Some are forced to live in the most horrid conditions as domestic sex slaves and house workers. They can be subjected to legal beatings from their husbands or ritualistic murders, which are both condoned and encouraged by society. Even in cultures where women have obtained basic human rights, an undercurrent of sexism and inequality thrives among the population where there exist glass ceilings, unequal pay, and rampant gender specific violence that is widely ignored by authorities. The frequency of these acts aids considerably in a perceived normality. Then, the normality of discrimination, violence, and oppression toward women acts as justification to the oppressors.

The common attitude toward women becomes, "If women were not inferior, they would not be so easily dominated in every culture."

So, how did this way of thinking come into place? And where did this animosity between men and women come from? To answer those questions we must explore why oppressors feel the need to dominate and control another person or group. Then, their tactics, both physical and psychological, must be exposed. Lastly, the victims of oppression must unlearn the lessons they have been taught in a slavery mentality and act with a free mind. The greatest barrier in overcoming an oppressor is to be freed from the mind-set that the abuse is deserved. Women are conditioned to be victims of learned helplessness and feelings of worthlessness before birth so they will be receptive to oppression.

Cultures unjustly depict women as temptresses, easily corruptible, irrational, emotional, weaker, inferior beings. Pinpointing the exact position where this vicious character assassination began would be Adam in the Garden of Eden accusing his wife before God, claiming, "This woman you gave to be with me gave me the fruit and then I ate" (see Genesis 3:12). In that one statement Adam claimed that the woman in her nature had somehow tempted him, was easily corrupted by the deception of the snake (being led by irrational emotions), and was weaker and inferior, as though he had not sinned at all. These very accusations have followed women ever since. The Bible has been used as reinforcement for the very oppressive ideals of Adam. However, what is largely ignored is that when Adam spoke he had already sinned and eaten the fruit. And as a sinner he was prone to be a liar. Rather than truth, the spoken words of a sinner are believed to perpetuate the blatant misuse of the Bible.

The stereotype Adam created was maintained for every generation after the Fall of humanity, along with the blaming and shame attached to all women for being born female. Shaming the woman's identity is the first step in oppressing her. If the woman is presented as sinful in her very nature, then by nature men can deem that it is their responsibility to oppress women to have power over sin. To gain acceptance of this oppression, women themselves are made to believe that they are the cause for sin and that acting in ways that extend beyond cultural stereotypes will only result in more sin and suffering.

When women learn to accept the shame of being deemed sinful, they lose the will to stand against oppressors. They remain under the impression that acting on their own thoughts is what created the problems in the first place. Without the will to fight, conquering her becomes only a matter of having the will to do it. Eve sinned when she acted in her own mind because it was against what God had said. However, women thinking for themselves and sin are mutually exclusive. When Adam blamed Eve, on the other hand, he took those mutually exclusive events and made them interdependent. By attaching sin to a woman simply acting on her own, oppressors have created an unwinnable argument that can be relied upon no matter how illogical, cheap, unjust, or cruel.

Oppressive men justify their dominance based on the Adam argument—men must rule because it was a woman acting in a position above a man that resulted in sin. The fundamental flaw in the argument is that if men are chosen to be leaders by right of being male, then as leaders they would be personally responsible for the decisions of everyone under their care. Therefore, as a man, Adam would share all the guilt of sin for his failure to protect Eve. Blaming Eve would then be a sign of his deep personal weakness, and would negate his own argument that sin was her fault. That is the obvious illogical aspect of Adam's argument, yet this illogical argument continues to be used in defense of oppressing women. The oppressor's justification is the cheap cover of an unwinnable argument, like a witch hunt.

In a witch hunt, the trial of an accused witch could consist of her hands being bound and her being thrown into a river. If she did not drown, she was a witch and subject to punishment; her innocence could only be proven if she died. With Adam's argument, a woman can only be redeemed of her supposed sinful nature by being submissive to an oppressive culture, while standing against it acts as evidence that she disrespects authority and order. The clear manipulation of environment to exploit the results contributes to the systematic unjust treatment of women.

The lack of accountably empowers oppressors to freely express cruelty. The role of man as the provider is used to assume dominance. Provision can be withheld to make a woman destitute. Then, the woman's destitution will cause her to submit willingly to an oppressor or be left with the option to struggle physically, spiritually, emotionally, or financially. In either choice, her helplessness leads back to Adam's original argument. By submitting she is proven to be codependent upon male leadership; and by resisting her physical, spiritual, emotional, or financial struggle she proves that she needs men in order to not struggle—even though her struggle is the direct result of a male-manipulated environment.

So why is there such a concerted effort to control women? This question also has its root in the Garden of Eden. After creating Adam, God said that it was not good for man to be alone. God then created woman as a suitable counterpart to the man. Adam's side of this argument would make it appear that women were created as subordinates. However, she was created to help the man because God saw that the man needed help. If the man was perfectly whole on his own, God would not have created the female counterpart.

Before sin, when Adam met Eve, Genesis records that a man is supposed to leave his father and mother and cleave to his wife (Gen. 2:24). By declaring that a man is to cleave to his wife, Adam asserted his need for her. Now, with an inordinate need for her help, the man experienced a loss of control. Also, in response to her creation, another person would serve as a witness to actions that may have been otherwise unnoticed.

> Just as water reflects the face, so one human heart reflects another.
>   —PROVERBS 27:19, CJB

If Adam was imperfect in any way, Eve would be certain to be aware of it. Her presence alone created potential fear of exposure and loss of control.

Then, Adam sinned in eating the fruit on the forbidden tree. Although the woman was not irreproachable, Adam stood exposed in his own guilt. In order to lessen the blow of his poor leadership and fear of loss, an effort was contrived to delegitimize her position to deny his own accountability. Adam played the victim of a supposed mutual mistake when he failed to act when it was most needed. At will, Adam lifted his authority to blame Eve when things were going wrong, but then decided to take the authority back up when it was convenient to him in order to rule over her.

The man seeks to rule over the woman because he is still bound to his need for her help. One way to assure he would never be without her help is to dominate over her in every way. By assuming control over a woman, the man would be fulfilling his need for her without having to recognize her equal share as created in the image of God.

> So God created mankind in his own image, in the image of God he created them; male and female he created them.
>
> —GENESIS 1:27

The male's dominance in the situation shifts the roles to her needing him, when really God created her because *he* needs her. Rather than acting as a counterpart, the woman now functions as an enabler to oppression by becoming weak and conforming to the lie that she alone caused sin. With the man denying his culpability in sin, there is no expectation for him to change. The woman who has expectations of a man is branded unsubmissive. Then, the woman is tricked into submitting to an ungodly man as though this was the order to which life should be conformed.

However, the lie will be defeated by the truth. The truth has to be discovered through thorough investigations of Scripture, without the filter of Adam's contempt and character assassination. Scriptures that have been misused to oppress women must be exposed in their true meaning. Then, women must look at Scripture through the eyes that they are not intended to be in bondage. They must understand that they are not doomed to live under the curse of desiring their husband and him ruling over her. Through the redemption of Yeshua as Messiah, all curses are broken. Also, further hope lies ahead for the woman as the rest of the Bible's prophecies come to pass; she will learn that God intends to do a new thing, and women will ascend to the mighty.

Author's Note: This book is about a search for truth. In that search I found a source of empowerment for women through their Messiah, commonly referred to as Jesus. But as I searched the Hebrew roots of the Scriptures, I found the Hebrew roots of Messiah, and that His name is Yeshua, which means salvation and victory. Therefore, throughout this text, the Messiah Jesus will be referred to as Yeshua.

Chapter 1

STONEWALLING— THE FIRST SIN

*G*ENESIS CHAPTER 3 gives an account of how sin entered the world when Adam and Eve disobeyed God's order and ate the fruit from the forbidden tree, which caused death. Everyone has felt the sting of death in one way or another. When the events of why death exists are recalled, it appears that the Fall of man occurred at the hands of a woman. Eve, easily deceived, eats the fruit and then presents it as temptation to Adam, who then partakes in it. When Adam is questioned about his decision, he quickly defects to, "the woman gave it to me."

Over time this has been viewed as a plausible excuse. Male dominance is viewed as a way to keep men safe from being led astray by a beguiled woman. However, Adam was not deceived. He was with his wife during the entire incident, and instigated sin with passive-aggressive behavior.

> When the woman saw that the fruit of the tree was good for food and pleasing to the eye, and also desirable for gaining wisdom, she took some and ate it. She also gave some to her husband, who was with her, and he ate it.
> —GENESIS 3:6

Adam had been with her the entire time, witnessing the conversation between his wife and the snake, and did not speak up. In Genesis 2:15, God charged Adam to work in the garden. The Hebrew says specifically, לעבדה ולשמרה *(leauv'dah oo'lesamarh)*, which means to work and to guard. So when the snake was talking to Eve, Adam should have acted in some way to guard and uphold what God had said about not eating from the tree. However, Adam remained silent.

Adam's silence can be referred to as stonewalling. It is a term often used to describe the way a man can shut down emotionally in a relationship. The act of stonewalling includes behaviors such as ignoring, walking out on a conflict, or not speaking. Because Adam was stonewalling at the time the event occurred, his motives to eat are not as easily discerned as Eve's. However, time revealed Adam's character. His silence was actually the main initiator of sin and death being brought into the world.

The snake began his deception with a question: "Did God *really* say, 'You must not eat from any tree in the garden'?" (Gen. 3:1, emphasis added). This question was testing to see what the woman believed. She quickly responded with an explanation of how they were permitted to eat from all the trees except the tree in the center of the garden or they would die. Her response repeated what God had said, almost verbatim, except for the addition of "do not touch it." God never made any regulations about touching the tree in the center of the garden. This added statement was the first sign that a belief system divergent to the Word of God had been instilled.

Genesis chapter 2 described the creation history of humankind. God gave the order concerning the tree of knowledge of good and evil to Adam before Eve was ever created. After Eve was created, God did not repeat the order, so it can be concluded that Eve received her information concerning the tree from Adam. The addition of "do not touch it" seemed simply like an extra precaution, but it is the first instance of religious tradition being added to the Word of God. There can also be speculation that the inception of this religious ideal came from either party; however, from Genesis 3:6 it is known that Adam was there with Eve and did not object to her saying "don't touch it."

Next the serpent said, "It is not true that you will surely die." This should have been a major warning bell to Adam. By saying "It is not true," the serpent was stating directly that God was a liar. Adam's silence in the situation acted as agreement to what the snake was saying. In Genesis 3:12, Adam declares that he ate because the woman gave him the fruit, clearly displaying that he was not deceived. So by eating the fruit, Adam willfully exhibited his agreement that God was a liar. By simply remaining silent, Adam had moved from being a bystander to open rebellion against God.

When Adam finally spoke, his character was revealed:

> The man said, "The woman you put here with me—
> she gave me some fruit from the tree, and I ate it."
>
> —GENESIS 3:12

He accepted no accountably for his own actions in failing to guard, לשמרה *(lesamarh)*, the tree. By blaming Eve, it appeared that Adam expected God to only punish her. How did he move from saying, "This is the bone of my bone and the flesh of my flesh," to an outright condemnation of his wife? Adam's stonewalling was a passive-aggressive behavior that uses the other party's emotions as a weapon.

The emotion Eve probably experienced was confusion. She was hearing three different messages about the same topic. First, there was God's order, which she heard via Adam, saying "if you eat from this tree, you will die"; next, there was the snake saying, "you won't die"; and lastly, there was Adam standing with her silently giving conflicting signals. Adam had relayed God's message, but at some point there was also an additional piece of information—"don't touch it"—which could not be verified as true. Adam's silence gave no reinforcement as to which message to follow.

Now, Eve was left to decide for herself. She saw that the fruit was good for food and desirable for making one wise. God did not say that the fruit was not good for food or that it would not make her wise. So as the lust of the eye prevailed, there was a subtle truth to what the snake said. With Eve likely feeling confused about who was right, the desire to be wise seemed like a solution to the problem. After this, Adam ate the fruit, knowing that Eve had been deceived.

In Adam's response to God, saying, "This woman...," he was using her emotional journey of confusion and lust of the eye as a substitute for his actions in failing to guard, לשמרה *(lesamarh)*, the tree. His implication was that if this woman were not so emotional and unstable, sin would not have occurred. It also must be noted that it was God who created the woman, so not only was Adam blaming his wife, but he was also left-handedly blaming God for creating her.

Passive-aggressive offenders do not take responsibly for their actions. The goal of showing their hostility passively is to cover their motives. This was clearly displayed in the way Adam passively agreed with the snake by stonewalling Eve. Sin first begins in the mind. Yeshua gave an example of this in Matthew 5:27–28: "You have heard that it was said, 'You shall not commit adultery.' But I tell you that anyone who looks at a woman lustfully has already committed adultery with her in his heart." Before Adam ever ate the fruit, he had to think about it first, and had already rebelled against God in his heart.

The known facts are that Adam witnessed the entire conversation between Eve and the snake, and then after he ate the fruit he blamed Eve. An example of a similar situation would be a parent with two children who leaves the house to run some errands. The parent tells the older child to look after everything while he is gone and not to open the oven. After the parent has left, one of the neighborhood kids comes over knowing there is a cake in the oven and asks the younger of the two children if they can open the oven and eat the cake.

The younger child knows via a message from her older brother that she should not open the oven. The older sibling even said, "Don't touch the oven." However, the neighborhood kid says that the parent will not be mad if they just peek inside the oven to see if the cake is done. The older child stands right next to the younger in the kitchen not objecting. The younger child looks up to her older brother and takes the silence as confirmation that merely peeking inside the oven is permitted. She opens the oven, and suddenly the cake drops. When the parent comes back home and finds a flat cake, the older child quickly says the younger one did it.

Looking at the psychology of sibling rivalry, older children have a tendency to try to get the younger siblings into trouble. They have been around longer and have learned a few things about the world. There is also the dynamic of how for the first two or so years of his life, it was just him and his parents. Then out of nowhere a younger child comes along, and now he has to share the glory. In comparison, Adam's motive appears to be that of an older sibling seeking to get back at the younger sibling for simply existing.

In the anecdote of the children with the oven, notice how when the neighborhood kid arrived, the older sibling did not address his presence. Most parents would not agree to have another child over without supervision. In the same way, Adam did not address the presence of the snake.

In Genesis 2:19, yet still before Eve was created, it says that Adam named all the animals that God put before him. This means that the snake was put before Adam. The term *naming* is not exclusive to deciding what something is to be called, but also means to bestow honor or assign character. The word *snake* in Hebrew means one who hisses, a spell, or prognosticate. Hissing is a show of hatred, disapproval, condemnation, or force; a spell, akin to witchcraft, is rebellion; and something that is prognostic is an omen, or an indication of probable course of a disease. Genesis 3:1 described the snake as subtle and crafty, and Adam had met the snake before. The moment the snake began speaking, Adam, knowing the creature's nature, should have intervened. Instead, Adam used the nature of the snake as a catalyst for his evil intentions toward his wife.

The neighborhood kid conveniently comes over as soon as the parent leaves and immediately knows to speak to the youngest child about doing something they know should not be done. The older child in the situation, like Adam, had already showed some subtle signs of wanting to go beyond the boundary of the parent's authority and added a little to what the parent had said. "Don't touch the oven" seemed like a legitimate warning to the younger child. It may have even sounded similar to what the parent said. However, when the younger child put her hand on the bar to open it, immediately the precautions of the warning were mixed with confusion. If the younger child had touched a hot surface unit on the oven, there might have been a danger; but merely grasping the cool handle bar to pull the door open provided a danger-free situation. In the simple action of

touching the handle bar of the oven, the younger child
had proven in her mind that there was no danger in
touching the oven, so it could mean that there was also
no danger in opening it.

When Eve was struggling about what to do, she had
also been given conflicting information before. Adam
manipulated the situation with conflicting information,
making her predisposed to deception. He waited there
silently as the snake finished the work he started, and
watched her eat the fruit of death. Adam used her doubt,
something he instilled in her when he was relaying
God's order, to manipulate. When Adam potentially said,
"Don't eat it and don't touch it," which was Eve supposed
to trust more—the actual Word of God, "Don't eat it,"
or the religious aspect of it "Don't touch it"? And how
could she make the distinction?

Adam was silent so he could defect to saying, "I didn't
do anything wrong." Although Adam did eat the fruit,
he could even justify himself because he had upheld the
religious tradition of not touching the tree, since it was
Eve who had presented the fruit to him. God is the sovereign maker and giver of laws. The addition of "don't
touch it" to God's law concerning the tree was a sign
that Adam was already at odds with God's ability to
make law, feeling the need to create his own.

Adam had issues with God's authority and attempted
to manipulate the law to get his way. His blaming the
woman also reflects blame upon God for creating her. It
was God who said, "It is not good for man to be alone."
When God created them male and female, God saw that
it was good. So by saying it was solely the woman's fault
that he sinned, Adam was saying that it was not good

that she had been created. If Adam could prove that the woman in her existence was not good, he would therefore have cause to usurp the authority of God. The passive-aggressive motives of Adam's stonewalling were to murder his wife in order to test God.

When God created the woman, He took something out of Adam. The Hebrew word צלע *(t'sala)*, which is translated as "rib," can also mean "side," showing that a significant part of Adam was taken from him in the creation of woman. The Spirit of God, רוח *(ruach)*, is feminine. With God creating humankind in His image, the feminine part of Adam, who was in the spirit, was born in the flesh.

> So God created mankind in his own image, in the image of God he created them; male and female he created them.
>
> —GENESIS 1:27

The woman had a life-giving womb in the physical manifestation of flesh, the feminine spirit of God.

God said that He would make a fitting helper for man. Accompanying the word "helper" is the term נגד *(negad)*, which means to be a counterpart, strong support, or as a post to lean upon. The root word "helper" also means to be an adversary, to expose to or to stand boldly against as opposite. She was called woman because she was taken from man.

The construct of the female included the womb. Since woman was taken from man, it is reasonable to conclude that before her creation the man also possessed the womb physically or spiritually. Adam's actions in stonewalling can be an indication of jealousy towards his wife. In accusing his wife before God, perhaps Adam intended for God to give the womb back, or reclaim the strength that left him in her creation, or to eliminate the woman altogether.

Rather than having a direct standoff with God, Adam choose to passive aggressively undermine His Word, "It is not good for man to be alone." Adam deliberately allowed death to enter into the world to murder his wife. He stood there silently watching the snake deceive his wife so she would eat the fruit and die. However, after Eve ate the fruit, she did not collapse immediately. After Adam saw that Eve did not die instantly, the resentment between Adam and God fully manifested in the physical act of rebellion when Adam followed and ate the fruit.

When Adam was confronted about his current state of sin, Adam chose to abandon responsibility and blame Eve. Rather than upholding the Word of God and guarding and saving the world from death, Adam faltered.

> If you falter in a time of trouble, how small is your strength! Rescue those being led away to death; hold back those staggering toward slaughter. If you say, "But we knew nothing about this," does not he who weighs the heart perceive it? Does not he who guards your life know it? Will he not repay everyone according to what they have done?
> —PROVERBS 24:10–12

God saw what was in Adam's heart and repaid him in the way he deserved. All the ground was cursed because Adam ate from the tree God ordered him not to eat from. When speaking to Adam, God had said, "Because you followed your wife." Adam had followed his wife in the very snare he had set for her.

> Since they hid their net for me without cause and without cause dug a pit for me, may ruin overtake them by surprise—may the net they hid entangle them, may they fall into the pit, to their ruin
> —PSALM 35:7–8

Then, God made a covenant with Eve and with her seed:

> And I will put enmity between you and the woman, and between your offspring and hers; he will crush your head, and you will strike his heel.
> —GENESIS 3:15

God knew that Eve had been deceived, and He placed enmity between the two seeds so she would have the ability to recognize her enemy and not be deceived again. God also knew that Adam had betrayed her and failed to uphold his duty to guard the Word of God. Therefore, the duty to guard and contend with the snake and his seed was given to another. God did not make a covenant with Adam knowing murder was in his heart. The hope of humanity was for humanity to be continued without the corruption Adam created.

In Genesis 3:16, God told the woman that her desire would be after her husband and that he would rule over her. Desire is something that takes place in the mind. Eve knew very well that Adam had betrayed her unto death. However, his betrayal was also a form of rejecting her. When people experience rejection from an intimate partner, it actually binds the heart of that person to the one rejecting them. This drives the rejected person to seek solace from the person rejecting her despite the logic of how badly her intimate partner is treating her. This sets the stage for a cycle of emotional abuse.

When someone is involved in a relationship with an abuser, the mind will go into correction mode to compensate for the abuse. If the abuse is emotional and passive aggressive, as it was with Adam, then the mind seeks to be restored on an emotional level. As a result, Eve would seek comfort from Adam to correct the feelings of rejection. When God said that her desire would be after her husband, He was speaking in terms of the emotional bondage that was created by Adam's rejection of Eve. Adam could withdraw from her at any moment and stonewall at the most crucial moments of emotional need, then condemn her actions when she responded out of lack.

The root word for desire as used in this instance, שׁוּק *(sooqa)*, means to stretch out after, to run after, overflow, to give in abundance to. The more Adam stonewalled Eve, the more she would compensate by overflowing with affection for him. Also, in making a covenant with her seed, Eve would also need an impregnator of that seed. With Adam being the only human on the earth, in order for the human race to continue she would turn to him. Adam, as the abuser in the relationship, would continue in his sinful ways and use the emotional and physical tie he had to Eve as manipulation to rule over her. Adam would maintain an emotional distance from her, stonewalling, and the more she overflowed toward him, the more he would pull away.

Adam's passive-aggressive behavior could have likely resulted in Eve lashing out angrily, which Adam would once again use as a weapon to demoralize her character. Every argument could ultimately conclude with Adam continually blaming her for the downfall of humanity. Since Eve made the mistake of eating the fruit, she could also experience self-condemnation. She would constantly look to Adam to fill the lack of confidence she had in herself. Adam would then feed her more condemnation as his method of denial for the psychological abuse she was suffering.

By bringing into question the meaning for Eve's existence, feeding her the lie that she alone caused the downfall of humanity, Eve would have no source of confidence in herself. Every act of service Adam did would be viewed as a gift to her for having to tolerate her "flawed" character and existence. By turning God's words around, Adam had centered the control around making it appear that he was her sustenance and support for the woman's emotional needs as opposed to the woman being a support, נגד *(negad)*, to him. Although he ate the fruit, Adam could always claim that because Eve was deceived, she did not have a clear perspective on the situation to judge his character or the snake's. If Eve were to lash out at him, Adam could potentially use it to further prove his point that she was altogether flawed in her makeup, and too emotional to be discerning, decisive, or survive without his leadership.

If Eve ever stood up to Adam, he could withdraw even further, claiming that it was her pushing the forbidden fruit onto him that caused all their problems in the first place. He could continue to deny his betrayal of her under the guise of her deception. Emotions cloud judgment. Therefore, anytime Eve sought Adam out emotionally, he could present it as evidence that her thinking is flawed and clouded. Adam would never trust her judgment or respect her as an equal sharer of the world. This would begin a cycle of rejection where Eve would continue to seek comfort from a man who would stonewall and use her desire for him to manipulate, dominate, and rule over her.

God made a sovereign choice to create Eve. Adam had an issue with God's ability to rule, so he used the evil nature of the snake to sabotage his wife. The only way Adam could exert his own authority was through condemnation. Ruling over his wife served as compensation for feeling helpless over the sovereign authority of God. This is why through Adam everyone is connected to condemnation.

> The judgement followed one sin and brought condemnation.
> —ROMANS 5:16, NCPE

There is no scripture that states that Adam repented or showed any remorse for his actions, or even thanked God in any form. Genesis chapter 5 has an account of the generations after Adam down to Noah. By the time Noah came along, the world was filled with violence to the point where God was moved to destroy it.

In typical thinking, based on how long people usually live today, we do not overtly recognize the intimate knowledge and interactions Adam had with these subsequent generations of men. But Adam lived for a total of 930 years. He was alive all the way into the generation of Lamech, which is only one generation away from Noah and the Flood.

Adam was a father to all these men, who filled the world with violence, and he knew them. Only by exception was God sought out; the vast majority were corrupt. In following the murder spirit that Adam had toward his wife, as men began to fill the earth, they filled it with violence.

> The LORD saw how great the wickedness of the human race had become on the earth, and that every inclination of the thoughts of the human heart was only evil all the time.
>
> —GENESIS 6:5

A tree is known by its fruit.

> By their fruit you will recognize them. Do people pick grapes from thornbushes, or figs from thistles? Likewise, every good tree bears good fruit, but a bad tree bears bad fruit. A good tree cannot bear bad fruit, and a bad tree cannot bear good fruit.
>
> —MATTHEW 7:16–18

The fruit of Adam is obvious within the first generation. His son Cain murdered his own brother. When God asked Cain where his brother was, Cain's response is similar to Adam's answer for sin in the garden: "'I don't know,' he [Cain] replied. 'Am I my brother's keeper?'"

(Gen. 4:9). Cain's immediate denial and shift of responsibility is exactly what his father did when he blamed Eve as though he had nothing to do with the forbidden fruit being eaten.

Cain carried the same jealous nature as his father, Adam. Cain was angry because God accepted the sacrifice of his brother. The major difference between Cain and Adam was that Cain's violence manifested openly rather than passively. This is because hidden sin increases over the generations.

> And the LORD passed before him and proclaimed, "The LORD, the LORD God, merciful and gracious, longsuffering, and abounding in goodness and truth, keeping mercy for thousands, forgiving iniquity and transgression and sin, by no means clearing the guilty, visiting the iniquity of the *fathers* upon the children and the children's children to the third and the fourth generation."
> —EXODUS 34:6–7, NKJV, EMPHASIS ADDED

Note: Other translations of this scripture say "parents," but the Hebrew specifies "fathers."

Adam's hidden agenda to murder his wife was confirmed when the iniquity of his son Cain recycled itself in the murder of his brother. The iniquity passes from the father, because it was Adam who caused sin to enter into the world. Adam's hidden motives function the same way iniquity does. Iniquity is hidden sin that is passed on generationally. Also, because God made a covenant with the seed of the woman, iniquity could only have come through the father.

On account of Adam's sin, the ground was cursed. It was cursed because of the defilement that death causes on the land. Bloodguilt for murder defiles the land.

> Do not pollute the land where you are. Bloodshed pollutes the land, and atonement cannot be made for the land on which blood has been shed, except by the blood of the one who shed it.
> —NUMBERS 35:33

This occurred dramatically after Cain murdered his brother.

> Now you are under a curse and driven from the ground, which opened its mouth to receive your brother's blood from your hand. When you work the ground, it will no longer yield its crops for you. You will be a restless wanderer on the earth.
> —GENESIS 4:11–12

Everywhere Cain wandered became a desert, in response to the bloodguilt. Adam initiated the curse. Although Eve did not die immediately, the ground fell under a curse because it would eventually receive her blood and that of everyone else who was born.

Adam stonewalled, which made his motives for allowing the snake to deceive his wife not easily seen. But Adam can be known by his fruit, as a murderer. The fruit of Adam was Cain, who was a murderer. Then the fruit of Cain produced even more callous murders. Lamech, a descendant of Cain, bragged to his wives that he killed a man for merely wounding him in Genesis 4:23.

God put enmity between the seed of the woman and the seed of the snake, Satan. How would it be possible for the snake to get a seed? So far the only people killing are the seed of Adam.

Genesis 3:1 described the snake as subtle (ASV). By stonewalling his wife when she really needed him to speak up, Adam was subtle in his manipulation.

Yeshua referred to people as snakes:

> You snakes! You brood of vipers! How will you
> escape being condemned to Hell?
> —MATTHEW 23:33, NCPE

When a person becomes a son of a snake, it is evident in the fruit that is produced in life as well as the actions of the subsequent generations. Did placing enmity between the seed mean that Adam had taken on the nature of the snake and was Eve's enemy?

The term that is translated as "helper," נגד *(negad)*, has a root in being an opposition to. Why would God create Eve to potentially be an adversary to her husband? Perhaps because God had already seen what was in the heart of Adam and needed to separate the life-giving womb from him. *Negad* also means to expose. Perhaps Eve was placed there to expose the wickedness in Adam's heart. Adam may have known this, which would be another cause for him to betray and try to dominate his wife.

Later, after the fall of humanity, Eve also saw the fruit of Adam:

> And Adam knew his wife again, and she bore a
> son and named him Seth, "For God has appointed

another seed for me instead of Abel, whom Cain
killed."

—GENESIS 4:25, NKJV

In that simple statement, Eve made a distinction
between Abel and Cain. The seed of Seth was a substitute for Abel. She spoke as though she did not consider Cain her son. Based on just the actions of the
children, she knew that Seth was of her seed whereas
Cain was not. An example of this same distinction is
made in Romans chapter 9 where it describes the difference between Jacob and Esau. Although Jacob and
Esau were conceived in a single act, as fraternal twins,
God chose Jacob to be His heritage. In the same way,
Cain and Seth had the same father and mother, but it
was the descendants of Seth who were the promised
seed of the woman.

All of Cain's descendants were wiped out in the Flood,
and humanity was continued through the line of Seth,
through the descendants of Noah. However, as Noah's
children multiplied, they repeated the same pattern of
sins. Thus the genealogical line from which the seed of
the woman would come was refined even further. God
made a covenant with Abraham in Genesis 12:7: "The
LORD appeared to Abram and said, 'To your offspring I
will give this land.'"

The Book of Galatians specifically describes the nature
of the seed of this covenant:

> The promises were spoken to Abraham and to his
> seed. The Scripture does not say "and to seeds,"

meaning many people, but "and to your seed,"
meaning one person, who is Messiah.

—GALATIANS 3:16, NCPE

This was fulfilled with the Virgin Birth. Mary, who
was a descendant of Seth, Noah, Abraham, Isaac, Jacob,
and other covenanted people, begot the Messiah. The
Virgin Birth represents how God made a covenant
directly with the woman. Mary was impregnated by
the Spirit of God. Man was not involved in the concep-
tion of the Messiah, and therefore the iniquity that is
passed from the father did not corrupt Him. This is why
Yeshua is referred to as the second Adam. The difference
between Seth and Cain foreshadowed how God would
redeem humanity from the curse Adam brought upon it
by allowing sin to enter the world.

Adam became spiritually dead because of his willful
rebellion. In making a covenant with the seed of the
woman, humanity became a widow to its first husband—
Adam, condemnation, and death—then remarried to
another, Yeshua, who is salvation and life.

> Do not be afraid; you will not be put to shame. Do
> not fear disgrace; you will not be humiliated. You
> will forget the shame of your youth and remember
> no more the reproach of [being widowed]. For your
> Maker is your husband—the LORD Almighty is his
> name—the Holy One of Israel is your Redeemer;
> he is called the God of all the earth.
>
> —ISAIAH 54:4–5

The Hebrew root word of "widowed" is אלם *(alma)*,
which means to be a desolate place or bereaved. It is also

akin to being discarded, forsaken, or divorced, terms that are used interchangeably in certain instances. The Scripture says that God hates divorce. Many theologies do not allow divorce, yet it is mentioned in the Scripture. What is the cause of this?

> Yeshua replied, "Moses permitted you to divorce your wives because your hearts were hard. But it was not this way from the beginning."
>
> —MATTHEW 19:8, NCPE

In the beginning they were created male and female. It is only when the man allows his heart to become hardened that divorce is allowed. By stonewalling, blaming, and betraying his wife, Adam set up humanity to carry the generational iniquity of divorce.

> You ask, "Why?" It is because the LORD is the witness between you and the wife of your youth. You have been unfaithful to her, though she is your partner, the wife of your marriage covenant.
>
> —MALACHI 2:14

The Hebrew root word for "unfaithful," בגד *(bagad)*, means to cover, to act covertly, to pillage, deal treacherously, offend, to act deceitfully. By stonewalling, Adam was covering his actions, being deceitful about his intentions for his wife, and dealing treacherously with life and death. When the Scripture says that God hates divorce, He hates that a man would rise against his own flesh, taking on the snake nature of deceit and subtly breaking apart the union He created in knitting them together as male and female. God is grieved over His creation being subject to death and separation. Romans 8:20 says, "For the creation was subjected to frustration, not by its own choice, but by the will of the one who subjected it." Divorce is allowed so that the victim of the faithless may be set free and redeemed by the righteous.

When Yeshua described His return, He said it would be like a groom coming to get a bride. The feminine term "bride" does not mean that only women will be saved, but that the connection to the Messiah is feminine because of the promise God made to Eve that the seed of the woman would overcome sin.

In the letters Paul wrote to the Corinthians, he said that the head of the wife is her husband, but also he wrote in 1 Corinthians 11:11–12, "Nevertheless, in the Lord woman is not independent of man, nor is man independent of woman. For as woman came from man, so also man is born of woman. But everything comes from God." This is to show how neither can lord over the other, because although the man was given authority, he can only maintain his authority through the seed of the woman.

Adam was uncaring toward his wife, blamed her for his sin, allowed harm to come to her in pursuit of his selfish gain or vendetta, ignored problems, stonewalled his wife, used emotions for manipulation and control, and was a complete and utter failure in fulfilling his task to guard the tree. Compare these qualities to those of Yeshua, the seed of the woman. Yeshua loved so strongly that He was willing to lay down His life for others. He took on the sins of others as opposed to blaming them for sin. All who call upon Him can lay all their burdens upon Him instead of Yeshua laying His upon people. He came to people with truth and as a servant rather than as a domineering tyrant. Yeshua opened the path to the tree of life rather than closing it down.

> As for husbands, love your wives, just as the Messiah loved the Messianic Community, indeed, gave himself up on its behalf.
> —EPHESIANS 5:25, CJB

To love means that the husband will possess the qualities of Yeshua as opposed to the stonewalling, murderous qualities of Adam. Therefore, if the husband does not have these qualities, he nullifies all authority he is given—the same way Adam handed all his authority over to Satan when he ate the fruit. Yeshua's sacrifice eradicated sin and broke all curses. The curse of the woman desiring a husband who has rejected her and God was also broken, because he can hold no authority over her without being connected to the Messiah. Hence a woman is under no obligation to follow a husband who stonewalls, dishonors, or does not love her, because when he does these things he fails to provide for his family.

> Anyone who does not provide for their relatives, and especially for their own household, has denied the faith and is worse than an unbeliever.
> —1 TIMOTHY 5:8

A woman should not be held in bondage because of a husband's failure to uphold his responsibilities.

> But if the unbeliever leaves, let it be so. The brother
> or the sister is not bound in such circumstances;
> God has called us to live in peace.
>
> —1 CORINTHIANS 7:15

Misogynistic viewpoints of Scripture that blame Eve for sin entering the world are in connection with Adam and condemnation. Those who hold these viewpoints are cycling the curse of Adam and death, which estranges them from the salvation that God promised through the seed of the woman, Messiah. The greatest act of stonewalling continuing in the present condition of the body of believers is the denial of the curse of Eve being broken. Men continue to subjugate their wives in the name of God in the same way Adam sought to rule over his wife.

Adam said, "This woman you gave to be with me…" as though claiming possession of her. He used the word נתת *(natata)* to describe his relationship with Eve, which means "gave," or "subject." This is contrary to the way God created Eve, as a support, mate, counterpart, or opposition *(negad)*. In connection to the woman's curse to desire after Adam is the value message that Adam placed on the woman as a possession. Misogynists continue to focus on the curse in their understanding of a woman's place in a relationship.

Women are no longer sufferers desiring their husbands but are free from condemnation, and outpour to God as their new husband, redeemed by Yeshua. Yeshua is the mediator between God and all humanity, and therefore women can seek their identity from God, being restored as a counterpart *(negad)* and no longer receiving the lie

Adam has told them. It is the woman's place to contend with the man if he is ungodly, as she was created to do, or to support the man if he is godly.

When the Scripture says she is to submit, it does not mean she is to be codependent, but a support. A support uses strength. Adam uses condemnation to place the woman under a curse in which her identity is defined as weak and in need of a man to support her. However, when women recognize their identity, they receive the message from God about who they are. They are the strength and support to the man when he is following Yeshua, and a contender and opposition to the man if he is going astray.

The first sin involved a man stonewalling to manipulate, control, and redefine the parameters of the relationship between the man and his wife, and deny the feminine aspect of God as being valid. Similar sin involves men continuing to stonewall the truth about the woman's identity to further manipulate and control. Learning from Eve's mistake, and by becoming redeemed through Yeshua, women can stand firm in the position that they are not to blame for sin and are no longer victims to a curse, stonewalling, and condemnation.

Chapter 2

RESPECT—A WOMAN'S PLACE

The LORD will make you the head, not the tail. If you pay attention to the commands of the LORD your God that I give you this day and carefully follow them, you will always be at the top, never at the bottom.

—DEUTERONOMY 28:13

*T*HE BODY OF believers is meant to be the head and not the tail, yet the body of believers is dying. The youth are going astray. The fastest growing faith is Islam. Growth in congregations consists mostly of people moving from one congregation to another

27

rather than nonbelievers becoming believers. There is no distinction between the world and the body of believers. Many factors contribute to the lack of power among believers, but one key issue is respect.

Often in congregations women are not respected and are excluded from roles in leadership. A woman who is empowered or seeks to be empowered is deemed to be a Jezebel, rebellious, or of loose moral values. Scriptures are typically quoted in relation to such women, intending to put them back in their place. The Scripture says that men are to be respected, but is that relationship of respect meant only to go one way?

The Book of Acts describes a rapidly growing number of Jewish people who were followers of "the way," who trusted in Yeshua as the Messiah. The apostles had power to heal the sick, raise the dead, and lead people to the truth. The key to their success in spreading the gospel was respect.

> Continuing faithfully and with singleness of purpose to meet in the Temple courts daily, and breaking bread in their several homes, they shared their food in joy and simplicity of heart, praising God and having the respect of all the people. And day after day the Lord kept adding to them those who were being saved.
>
> —ACTS 2:46–47, CJB

The early body of believers had the respect of all the people, and continually added to their numbers daily, which is a stark contrast to the believers of today. Today, believers are divided into many factions and denominations. Then, they are further divided by gender. There is no respect within denominations nor within individual congregations. During the time of the Acts of the Apostles, people witnessed miracles and were healed of physical afflictions. The act of respecting one another correlates to active healings and miracles taking place.

A common form of disrespect in the church is discrimination against women. This bias is justified by the abuse of selective scriptures. One of the most frequently abused scriptures is 1 Corinthians 14:34–35: "Women should remain silent in the churches. They are not allowed to speak, but must be in submission, as the law says. If they want to inquire about something, they should ask their own husbands at home; for it is disgraceful for a woman to speak in the church." By abusing this scripture, the message is sent that God is ashamed of women. Male leadership would be justified in favoritism based on sex, believing that women have no place to think or have a voice. The abuse this creates also puts an unwarranted focus on male favoritism that would automatically trump any feminine intelligence. If this was the intended use of the scripture in Corinthians, then questions such as "What if the husband does not learn as quickly as the wife does?" would have to be addressed. It would imply that all men learn faster and have greater understanding of the Scripture than all women. That is simply untrue.

Paul was writing a letter to the Corinthians about the proper way to run their congregations. The quote from 1 Corinthians 14:34–35 is a concept that was put forth by the Corinthians in their letters to him. Paul quotes their perception before he replies with the truth in the very next verse: "Or did the word of God originate with you? Or are you the only people it has reached?" (v. 36). This verse is a rebuke. In the letter the Corinthians had written to Paul, they said, "as also the law says." The law does not say that women are not permitted to speak. The Corinthians had created their own doctrine, thus preventing women from speaking during congregational meetings. The question "Did the word of God originate with you?" is to show them that they cannot create manmade rules in the name of God. Abusing Scripture and creating rules and calling it the Word of God is blasphemy, because it adds to the original Word of God.

> Do not add to what I command you and do not subtract from it, but keep the commands of the LORD your God that I give you.
> —DEUTERONOMY 4:2

The Scripture does not conflict itself. Neither does Paul conflict himself in the letters that he wrote.

> I am introducing to you our sister Phoebe, *shammash* of the congregation at Cenchrea, so that you may welcome her in the Lord, as God's people should, and give her whatever assistance she may need from you; for she has been a big help to many people—including myself.
> —ROMANS 16:1–2, CJB

The word *shammash* means "deacon," which is a form of leadership. Paul also charges the people to assist Phoebe in what she needs. To assist means to be of service to the person in charge. The Bible is not against female leadership, because it would be impossible for Phoebe to be a *shammash* if she were not permitted to speak.

When the letters Paul wrote were translated into English, the church had already established its traditions and regulations, which were not all accurate. Women were regarded with contempt and blocked from all forms of authority. Therefore, when the word *shammash* was used in reference to women, it was translated as "servant" as opposed to "deacon" when it referred to men.

> There is neither Jew nor Greek, slave nor free, male
> nor female, for you are all one in Messiah Yeshua.
> —GALATIANS 3:28, NCPE

The heritage and anatomy of a person does not change when he or she is immersed in the Messiah. This letter states that once a person is immersed in Yeshua, the Spirit of God will come upon them regardless of who they are. Disrespect toward women in the body of believers under the guise of a God-given order significantly blocks the movement of the Spirit of God.

The Holy Spirit descended during Shauvot (Pentecost) when the 120 people were praying in the Upper Room. The people became filled with the Spirit, and each one started speaking in tongues. According to Acts 2:8–11, in Jerusalem at the time were "Parthians, Medes and Elamites; residents of Mesopotamia, Judaea and Cappadocia, Pontus and Asia, Phrygia and Pamphylia, Egypt and the parts of Libya near Cyrene; visitors from Rome (both Jews and converts to Judaism); Cretans and Arabs." The people were amazed that all could understand their own language being spoken to the mixed crowd. After seeing this miracle and hearing the testimony of Peter, three thousand people were saved. The people praying in the Upper Room included women. If women were not permitted to speak, then the Holy Spirit, from God, would not have come upon them.

When Peter explained to the crowd what was happening, he quoted a scripture from the Book of Joel: "And afterward, I will pour out my Spirit on all people. Your sons and daughters will prophesy, your old men will dream dreams, your young men will see visions." (Joel 2:28). After the people accepted this testimony and were immersed, many miracles and signs took place. People from many different races came together and respected each other. Disrespect toward women in the body of believers is really disrespect toward God and His Word, which gives women authority. This may be part of the reason why miracles and healings in congregations are rare.

Without miracles there are no signs among believers that separate them from people of any other religion. Signs are a very important part of ministering in the name of Yeshua.

> Calling together the Twelve, Yeshua gave them power and authority to expel all the demons and to cure diseases; and he sent them out to proclaim the Kingdom of God and to heal.
> —Luke 9:1–2, cjb

> And these signs will accompany those who believe: In my name they will drive out demons; they will speak in new tongues; they will pick up snakes

with their hands; and when they drink deadly
poison, it will not hurt them at all; they will place
their hands on sick people, and they will get well.

—MARK 16:17–18

Jews demand signs and Greeks look for wisdom

—1 CORINTHIANS 1:22

Praying and having those prayers answered is also
directly related to how people interact with one another,
particularly husbands and wives.

You husbands, likewise, conduct your married
lives with understanding. Although your wife may
be weaker physically, you should respect her as
a fellow-heir of the gift of Life. If you don't, your
prayers will be blocked.

—1 PETER 3:7, CJB

God does not hear the prayers of a husband who disrespects his wife.

During the time of the early believers, the apostles
would pray and get immediate results. Today people
pray barely expecting an answer, let alone healing the
blind, lame, or crippled. There are countless prayers that
go up to God for healing or salvation that do not see any
return. This is because the level of disrespect toward
women in the body of believers is so high that the
prayers are not being heard. Without a healthy prayer
life there is no communication between people, the
Messiah, and God that would prompt signs or miracles.

A healthy prayer life is indicative in part of the relationship of respect as equals between men and women in the body of believers.

Disrespect toward women often takes place within married life. In Paul's letter to the Ephesians, he wrote that wives should submit to their husbands. This scripture is often used as a means to support a solely male-dominated organization. However, it is written in the preceding verse, "Submit to one another in fear of the Messiah" (Eph. 5:21, CJB). To submit to one another means that submission is not one-sided. The next verses in Ephesians give the example of how a wife submits by respecting her husband and following him the way she would the Messiah, while the husband submits to his wife by loving and providing for her the way he would for himself.

Submission also does not mean blind obedience to orders. The husband is not meant to give orders, but to lead in a compassionate, godly way.

> Wives, submit yourselves to your husbands, as is fitting in the Lord.
> —COLOSSIANS 3:18

The phrase "as fitting in the Lord" implies that there is a level of discretion in following the leadership of a husband. If the husband goes astray, the wife has the right to stand for righteousness. One example of this going wrong is Ananias and his wife, Sapphira.

Ananias sold some land but held back some of the money, with his wife's knowledge. When he presented his deception to Peter, he was called out on lying to the Holy Spirit and immediately fell down dead. Later, when Sapphira came before Peter, she followed in her husband's deception and was subject to the same penalty. Sapphira had the opportunity to repent on her own accord, but she chose to submit in a way that was not appropriate in the Lord. This cost Sapphira her life. If this occurred all in the name of submission, then it would give a husband unbending power to take the life of his wife.

Certain theologies teach that women must submit at all costs, ignoring the responsibility of leaders to be righteously submitted to God and the woman's ability to distinguish right from wrong. In this way even abuse can be justified, saying that the woman has to submit to it to be a godly wife. It is written in Deuteronomy 6:16, "Do not put the LORD your God to the test." Therefore, if God, who is ever compassionate and forgiving, is not to be put to the test, why is it justifiable for women to be constantly put to the test by neglectful or abusive husbands?

> He writes the same way in all his letters, speaking in them of these matters. His letters contain some things that are hard to understand, which ignorant and unstable people distort, as they do the other Scriptures, to their own destruction.
>
> —2 PETER 3:16

Uninstructed and unstable people distort the Scriptures to suit their misogyny. This is destructive to the people themselves and to the spreading of the gospel. Proverbs 26:9, "Like a thornbush in a drunkard's hand is a proverb in the mouth of a fool," reiterates the repercussions of a fool quoting Scripture out of context.

Yeshua said in Matthew 20:26–27, "whoever wants to become great among you must be your servant, and whoever wants to be first must be your slave" Therefore, a husband who leads becomes subservient to his wife, and by serving and submitting to a husband, a wife exhibits leadership in the relationship. This is how equality is established in the relationship, rather than men lording over their wives or wives domineering over husbands. Without including Ephesians 5:21 in the relationship between husbands and wives, it would appear that the Scripture is against women, and men have unquestioned authority. When the relationship between husbands and wives is taught, Ephesians 5:21 is not always included.

> But Yeshua called them and said, "You know that among the Goyim, those who are supposed to rule them become tyrants, and their superiors become dictators."
>
> —MATTHEW 20:25, CJB

A husband who demeans his wife in her service to him is not leading by the authority of God, but is acting as a pagan master. So the power leaves that relationship. Then, since each person constitutes parts of the one body of believers, the entire body loses power. The teaching of one-sided submission spilled over into how women are viewed in all walks of life.

In the workplace, specifically during the 1940s in the United States, women were often promoted only within a glass ceiling to force them to be subservient to all men. Most men felt as though they were biblically justified in their discriminatory actions. In reaction to this, women who fought for equal opportunities and pay were obliged only when the nation strayed from its traditional values. As a result, when movements are made for revival there is strong resistance from women or other groups who were denied their basic rights, from the misrepresented teachings of a fallen church.

> For Scripture says, "Do not muzzle an ox while it is treading out the grain," and "The worker deserves his wages."
> —1 TIMOTHY 5:18

The masculine language refers to both sexes. So it goes against Scripture to withhold a person's wages. Yet, the traditional values held by believers are contrary to what the Scriptures say. Had the body of believers maintained respect for women and paid them equally, like they were supposed to, we may not have seen such a movement to stray from biblical teachings.

Yeshua taught that when He returned it would be like a Bridegroom coming for a bride. The body of believers is meant to be ambassadors of the returning kingdom of God. If women are commonly disrespected in their marriages, then the believers are doing a poor job when it comes to being ambassadors of the kingdom of God. Fornication among nonbelievers, and even believers, is typically the first topic that people want to address. People are encouraged to get married and end sexual sin—but unsuccessfully, due to what marriage has come to represent.

It is difficult to look forward to the coming of a divine Bridegroom when the bridegrooms on earth treat their brides with such scorn. Rarely does a man view himself as a bride when it comes to a wedding. The closest understanding men have of what it means to be a bride is their wives. Since many men are so separated from their wives because of disrespect, there is significant lack of understanding of what it means to be the bride of Messiah; hence, husbands who disrespect their wives further separate themselves from Yeshua.

Respect for a woman also includes respecting her in a place of authority. In the Book of Judges, Deborah was a prophet and a judge over all Israel, and was specifically raised to authority by God: "Then the LORD raised up judges, who saved them out of the hands of these raiders" (Judg. 2:16). Deborah had a husband, yet she was the leader, and he did not contradict her authority (Judg. 4:4–5). For a woman to lead an entire country as a judge, she would have to exercise authority over men.

Paul writes in 1 Timothy 2:12, "I do not permit a woman to teach or to assume authority over a man; she must be quiet." It must be noted that in this scripture Paul is only giving his opinion. This is why it states "I do not permit," as opposed to "God does not permit." The continuation of this verse gives his reason for this opinion: "she is to remain at peace." Paul was merely suggesting to not burden women with the responsibility of leadership.

Being a leader means the possibility of giving up one's life for another; a role that he felt suited men because Adam was created first. It also makes the distinction that Eve was deceived, whereas Adam willingly sinned, having full knowledge of what he was doing, placing more blame on the man for the first sin as opposed to the woman. However, the current body of believers does not recognize prohibiting women from teaching is an opinion, nor do they recognize the reason for that opinion. It has come to mean that every man, regardless of his spiritual state, is free to ignore women.

The way this scripture is interpreted in the current body of believers, hypothetically a man who just got saved, and may still be backsliding, could walk into a congregation and be placed at a higher level of authority than a virtuous, God-fearing, well-established, believing woman. This is precisely what happens in churches, which is why there are many incompetent leaders who become stumbling blocks for nonbelievers to come to Yeshua.

> Anyone who lives on milk, being still an infant, is not acquainted with the teaching about righteousness. But solid food is for the mature, who by constant use have trained themselves to distinguish good from evil.
>
> —HEBREWS 5:13–14

Deborah was responsible for judging Israel because she was mature in her trust in God and knew His Word.

The body of believers is at a disadvantage because mature, knowledgeable people are excluded from leadership because they are women, while milk-drinking babies may be given positions because they are men. The blanket sentiment that women cannot lead goes against Scripture. God raises leaders, and fighting against the one whom God calls, even if it is a woman, is the same as fighting God.

> Let everyone be subject to the governing author-
> ities, for there is no authority except that which
> God has established. The authorities that exist
> have been established by God. Consequently,
> whoever rebels against the authority is rebelling
> against what God has instituted, and those who
> do so will bring judgment on themselves.
>
> —Romans 13:1–2

Another scripture that is abused in order to condemn women is in Isaiah: "Youths oppress my people, women rule over them. My people, your guides lead you astray; they turn you from the path." (Isa. 3:12). The religious establishment claims that female leaders inherently lead the people following them astray. However, this scrip-ture describes the spiritual state of Israel before they went into captivity.

When it says that youths will oppress them, the Hebrew word in the text is "infant." It does not liter-ally mean that babies are the leaders. The use of the term "infant" is a Hebrew idiom describing the leaders as immature and lacking knowledge of the ways of God. The feminine context of "women ruling over them" in the Hebrew is a reference to the leaders being effemi-nate. The term "effeminate" has undertones of being feminine, but it is clear that the act of being effemi-nate and being feminine are not the same. Effeminate leaders are leaders who are weak, corruptible, or possibly homosexual.

There are many examples in the Scriptures of how a word from God came directly to a woman rather than her husband, such as Samson's mother, Hannah, and Rebekah. Samson's mother was spoken to by an angel who told her she would conceive, and that her son would be a Nazirite from the womb. When she told her husband, he prayed and the word and instructions were confirmed. Hannah, the mother of Samuel, prayed directly to God and received a son. Rebekah, one of the matriarchs of the nation of Israel, was told by God about the two nations that were in her womb.

Many of the followers of Yeshua were women:

> After this, Yeshua traveled about from one town and village to another, proclaiming the good news of the kingdom of God. The Twelve were with him, and also some women who had been cured of evil spirits and diseases: Mary (called Magdalene) from whom seven demons had come out; Joanna the wife of Cuza, the manager of Herod's household; Susann; and many others. These women were helping to support them out of their own means.
>
> —LUKE 8:1–3, NCPE

Not only were there women followers, but they had their own source of income to help Yeshua in His ministry. This is a far cry from women being completely dependent on their husbands for income and barred from the workplace, as certain religious sects teach. Rachel worked as a shepherd. The woman in Proverbs chapter 31 was a businesswoman and bought land. There were also women who worked in the reconstruction of the temple during the time of Ezra and Nehemiah (Neh. 3:12).

When Yeshua revealed Himself as the Messiah, He revealed it to a woman. His disciples were amazed that He would even speak to a woman (John 4:27). This took place during the time when women lived completely separate lives from men. At the temple there was a partition to divide the women's side from the men's side, and this same type of partition was placed in synagogues. Talking to a woman was seen as lowly, unholy, or forbidden in some cases. Some churches of today carry on the tradition of being offended by women, dividing between men's and women's sections of the congregation, and excluding women from public reading of the word. This is the opposite of how Yeshua treated women.

> As Yeshua and his disciples were on their way, he came to a village where a woman named Martha opened her home to him. She had a sister called Mary, who sat at the Lord's feet listening to what he said.
>
> —LUKE 10:38–39, NCPE

This was a radical move, for a woman to sit and listen to a teaching among men. As the story went on, Martha wanted her sister, Mary, to help her in the kitchen. But rather than Yeshua commanding Mary to return to distaff, Yeshua commended her for choosing the right thing by learning from Him. In the letter Paul wrote to Titus, women are told to take care of their homes, but taking care of the home was an authoritative charge in terms of management. It was not meant to be the sole purpose for a believing woman, as Yeshua made clear through Martha and Mary.

By very simple analysis of Scripture, and by reading in context, the Bible is found to be unbiased. Yet for centuries discrimination has prevailed among the body of believers. Why does this occur? The most obvious reason would be that the men in charge preferred a system that unquestionably put them on top. They were willing to sacrifice the truth and the countless number of souls who turned away because of their perversion, just to be placed at a higher position. They were willing to use the Word of God to oppress the people they were supposed to be helping.

When Satan tempted Yeshua, he came to Him with Scripture, the same way the leaders of some religious organizations have come to use Scripture as a free pass to promote the bondage and oppression of women. One of the most famous unchivalrous female Bible characters, Jezebel, used this same tactic. Jezebel wrote letters in the name of the king to falsely accuse someone of a crime, then used the Scripture to condemn him to death. "Jezebel" is often the term assigned to women who question. The men in authority claim that these "Jezebels" do not respect authority because they are controlling. But looking at the history, who is the Jezebel? Who is trying to control whom, and who is the one being disrespected?

Man-made doctrines have deemed that women are irrelevant and only have value when dominated by men. Many of these false teachings are based on a perversion of the Scriptures. Yeshua combated the perversion of the Scripture that Satan approached Him with by using the proper framework of the Scriptures and the whole truth.

The misuse of scriptures to stifle and disrespect women is a driving force in the lack of power in the body of believers. Many have turned to secularism to avoid the oppression of a dying church, while those within the body of believers continue to labor without the strong presence of God and His manifest miracles. God created humankind as male and female and intends for them to serve His purpose with mutual respect as one.

Chapter 3

INDECISIVE

*T*HE STORY OF Esther is about a young Jewish girl who was chosen to be queen of the ancient Persian Empire by King Ahasuerus (Xerxes). During this time, Haman, an Agagite, advanced in political position in the kingdom, and he used his power to try to commit genocide against the Jewish people. Queen Esther intervened on behalf of her people by going before the king with her unsolicited request; something she could have easily lost her life for. The Book of Esther is retold as a story of courage and the preservation of God's chosen people. However, there is also a valuable message that is often overlooked: Esther is the queen leading a military victory against an adverse and hostile enemy.

One of the reasons Esther may not have seemed like a military leader is because her actions came across as indecisive. In the middle of the conflict she cries, she uses very indirect communication signals, and her authority appears to defect to her cousin Mordecai during the combat. She exhibited all the typical stereotypes of why women are seen as weak leaders. But beneath her outward appearance of uncertainty there was a very strong, perceptive, sound-minded leader who overcame many obstacles and achieved a stunning victory over multiple adversaries.

The most obvious villain in the story was Haman. Haman, the Agagite, received authority from Ahasuerus, King of Persia, to destroy all the Jewish people.

> Then Haman said to King Xerxes, "There is a certain people dispersed among the peoples in all the provinces of your kingdom who keep themselves separate. Their customs are different from those of all other people, and they do not obey the king's laws; it is not in the king's best interest to tolerate them. If it pleases the king, let a decree be issued to destroy them, and I will give ten thousand talents of silver to the king's administrators for the royal treasury."
>
> So the king took his signet ring from his finger and gave it to Haman son of Hammedatha, the Agagite, the enemy of the Jews. "Keep the money," the king said to Haman, "and do with the people as you please."
>
> Then on the thirteenth day of the first month the royal secretaries were summoned. They wrote out in the script of each province and in the language of each people all Haman's orders to the king's satraps, the governors of the various

provinces and the nobles of the various peoples. These were written in the name of King Xerxes himself and sealed with his own ring. Dispatches were sent by couriers to all the king's provinces with the order to destroy, kill and annihilate all the Jews—young and old, women and children— on a single day, the thirteenth day of the twelfth month, the month of Adar, and to plunder their goods. A copy of the text of the edict was to be issued as law in every province and made known to the people of every nationality so they would be ready for that day.

The couriers went out, spurred on by the king's command, and the edict was issued in the citadel of Susa. The king and Haman sat down to drink, but the city of Susa was bewildered.

—ESTHER 3:8–15

After this order was decreed, the hope of the Jewish people relied upon Esther the queen interceding on behalf of her people. But mediating was not just a simple task of asking the king to rethink his decision. Approaching the king spontaneously meant death.

All the king's officials and the people of the royal provinces know that for any man or woman who approaches the king in the inner court without being summoned the king has but one law: that they be put to death unless the king extends the gold scepter to them and spares their lives. But thirty days have passed since I was called to go to the king.

—ESTHER 4:11

The king had also signed the decree into law, which meant it was unalterable.

> Now write another decree in the king's name in behalf of the Jews as seems best to you, and seal it with the king's signet ring—for no document written in the king's name and sealed with his ring can be revoked.
>
> —Esther 8:8

Under Persian law the king had absolute power over any and all decisions, whether they were made brashly, while the king was drunk, or contradictory to laws that were already in place. This tyrannical form of leadership was displayed in the way King Ahasuerus banished his first queen, Vashti.

> On the seventh day, when King Xerxes was in high spirits from wine, he commanded the seven eunuchs who served him—Mehuman, Biztha, Harbona, Bigtha, Abagtha, Zethar and Karkas—to bring before him Queen Vashti, wearing her royal crown, in order to display her beauty to the people and nobles, for she was lovely to look at. But when the attendants delivered the king's command, Queen Vashti refused to come. Then the king became furious and burned with anger.
>
> Since it was customary for the king to consult experts in matters of law and justice, he spoke with the wise men who understood the times and were closest to the king—Karshena, Shethar, Admatha, Tarshish, Meres, Marsena and Memukan, the seven nobles of Persia and Media who had special access to the king and were highest in the kingdom.

"According to law, what must be done to Queen Vashti?" he asked. "She has not obeyed the command of King Xerxes that the eunuchs have taken to her."

Then Memukan replied in the presence of the king and the nobles, "Queen Vashti has done wrong, not only against the king but also against all the nobles and the peoples of all the provinces of King Xerxes. For the queen's conduct will become known to all the women, and so they will despise their husbands and say, 'King Xerxes commanded Queen Vashti to be brought before him, but she would not come.' This very day the Persian and Median women of the nobility who have heard about the queen's conduct will respond to all the king's nobles in the same way. There will be no end of disrespect and discord.

"Therefore, if it pleases the king, let him issue a royal decree and let it be written in the laws of Persia and Media, which cannot be repealed, that Vashti is never again to enter the presence of King Xerxes. Also let the king give her royal position to someone else who is better than she. Then when the king's edict is proclaimed throughout all his vast realm, all the women will respect their husbands, from the least to the greatest."

The king and his nobles were pleased with this advice, so the king did as Memukan proposed. He sent dispatches to all parts of the kingdom, to each province in its own script and to each people in their own language, proclaiming that every man should be ruler over his own household, using his native tongue.

—ESTHER 1:10–22

The laws that the ancient Persians adhered to was called the Gentoo code. The Gentoo code contained all the protocols concerning every aspect of Persian life. According to this code, wives were to be secluded from the public view. Queens and women married to high-ranking officials were especially set apart from society. They were covered with veils to represent the hierarchy of being secluded from public view. King Ahasuerus's request for Vashti to appear before his guests to display her beauty was in direct contrast to Persian law.

Although his request was contradictory to the law that was already in place, the king's word could still be enforced and defiance punishable even if refusal was based on following the law. These types of contradictions showed how brutal and wicked the Persians were. Although Vashti was following the law by refusing to come, because she made the king mad, he banished her and issued a decree to put all women in their place. The next adversary for Esther to contend against was the religious and political system of Persia.

The kingdom was set up specifically so that no one could openly approach the king. The king also had a temperament of lashing out. The first military action on Esther's part was the diplomacy of how she approached the king. She used very indirect communication when she invited the king to a banquet:

> On the third day Esther put on her royal robes and stood in the inner court of the palace, in front of the king's hall. The king was sitting on his royal throne in the hall, facing the entrance. When he saw Queen Esther standing in the court, he was

pleased with her and held out to her the gold scepter that was in his hand. So Esther approached and touched the tip of the scepter.

Then the king asked, "What is it, Queen Esther? What is your request? Even up to half the kingdom, it will be given you."

"If it pleases the king," replied Esther, "let the king, together with Haman, come today to a banquet I have prepared for him."

"Bring Haman at once," the king said, "so that we may do what Esther asks."

—ESTHER 5:1–5

Esther's indirect communication comes across as weakness, but really it was a shrewd maneuver to overcome her third adversary, a temperamental husband. In modern cultures, problems that exist between husbands and wives are often attributed to communication barriers. Women are ascribed as being emotional and indirect, while men are seen as logical and decisive. However, many of these communication barriers exist as a result of Persian influences in the culture.

The interaction between King Ahasuerus and Vashti was very direct. He made a request, and with no explanation of her motives or second-guessing herself, Vashti said no. Vashti was punished severely for being direct with her husband. Today this punishment comes in the form of character assassination with accusations that a woman who is straightforward about what she wants does not respect her husband. The decree of King Ahasuerus that every man should be master in his own house, following Vashti's banishment, is used as reinforcement for this ideal.

The religious and political system of Persia made King Ahasuerus appear to be a victim of undue humiliation. As king, he was presented as having control over everything, with the ability to create his own laws and undermine preexisting laws. Making a request put the king in a position where someone else was in control. Then, having the request refused by his wife made the king appear out of control and weak, which threatened his rule. The king would need to compensate immediately to appear strong. Vashti then became the target of his need to compensate. To prove his point and assert his dominance, he would have to further limit his wife's ability to be in control. Therefore, his decree was intended to shift his fear of humiliation to her, causing her to fear what he would do if she humiliated him.

This feeds into a system of indirect communication. The wife is forced to communicate on a level that compensates for the husband's constant fear of humiliation. Esther coming to the king, even with a valid issue, would easily be construed as trying to undermine his authority. Hypothetically, Esther making a direct approach could sound like this:

SAMPLE DIALOGUE:

Esther approaches the king unsummoned. "Ahasuerus, I need to talk to you. You approved a decree for genocide. There isn't any evidence that Haman's accusations about the Jews being traitors are true, and you didn't investigate it at all. The decree includes murdering children and women, just over money. You need to rethink your decision-making process, especially the way you create drastic, irrevocable laws while drunk. And by the way, I'm a Jew. So you signed a decree to kill all my people. And you didn't even know that they're my people, because you only picked me based on looks."

The king responds, "I've been running this kingdom since long before you got here, and I don't need you telling me how to be king. I'll do whatever I want when I want regarding the people in my kingdom. I am the master of this house; you don't tell me what to do."

The king looks at Esther condescendingly, then motions to have the guards take her away and behead her.

The king's wanton acceptance of genocide was a valid issue he needed to be confronted about. Also, the king's lack of investigation into Haman's claims before choosing a side was foolish. Proverbs 18:17 says, "In a lawsuit the first to speak seems right, until someone comes forward and cross-examines." Many of the major decisions King Ahasuerus made were made at wine banquets. In the opening of the book, he had decreed 180 days of partying and flaunting his wealth. One hundred eighty days is half a year during which it was very unlikely that any problems in the kingdom would be addressed. Ecclesiastes 10:16 says, "Woe to the land whose king was a servant and whose princes feast in the morning." Although the king was in desperate need of correction, reproof had to be relegated to compliance with his fear of humiliation.

If Esther had used the above sample dialogue, it is doubtful that she would have gotten past, "I need to talk to you." Even an approach that was less confrontational might not have helped:

Sample Dialogue:

Esther approaches the king, unsummoned. "King Ahasuerus, I am a Jew, and a decree has been issued decreeing the genocide of my people. Please rescind it."

King Ahasuerus sits up straight in his throne. "That decree was for 330 tons of silver for the royal treasury. I'm doing everything I can to secure finances for this kingdom, and you stand here undermining me over the people who are traitors to my kingdom. And I'm master of this house; you don't tell me what to do."

The king looks at Esther condescendingly, then motions to have the guards take her away and behead her.

In the sample dialogues, the approach Esther used would be seen as combative or ungrateful. The only safe approach for Esther would be to ask the king something completely unrelated to what she really wanted so it could not be turned around as an attack against her. Although there are cultures that are not as extreme as Persia in stifling women's ability to speak to their husbands, there still exist social systems that restrict direct communication. Then, the complaint that follows is that women never say directly what they want, forcing men to guess.

Women's indirect communication inhibits their ability to address immediate problems. Then men can further justify a need to always be in leadership positions. However, indirect communication is an intentional bondage created with the purpose of making women appear weak. When the argument is presented, it is based on the concept of men operating on logic. Esther requested a banquet, which would seem trivial on the lists of priorities such as immediate danger, food, shelter, etc. With no prior knowledge of how the situation related to Esther, how could King Ahasuerus know the difference between a casual request for dinner and an urgent, life-saving genocide prevention banquet request?

By eliminating Esther's (or any woman's) ability to communicate directly, an unwinnable argument was created before anything had been said. If he responded poorly to the situation, he could fall back on the fact that he did not know that an invitation to a banquet meant "save my people"; or if she approached directly, he could find fault with the method of her approach, claiming disrespect. This is a problem present in many relationships between husbands and wives, where it is not truly an issue of how women communicate but of women not being received on the other side of the case.

Relationships between husbands and wives retain this same setup through the misuse of the respect teaching. It is biblical for a wife to respect her husband. But this respect is meant to be part of a mutual partnership of equals. Misuse of the husband's need for respect creates the circumstances for him to hide behind this need to avoid addressing areas where he is weak. A wife who is aware of a bad decision her husband has made has a responsibility to rebuke him for it. This goes back to the garden and the original purpose of God creating the woman: to contend against the man, נגד *(negad)*.

Correction is an uncomfortable state to be in. It sends messages of inadequacy, incompetence, and contempt. However, once the correction is received, the person grows and is better off than he was before. On the other hand, the fear of feeling inadequate will cause the one being corrected to become stuck in that phase and not move on to the fruit that correction brings. Misusing the need for respect censures the one doing the correcting, and the one who needs correcting is not corrected. The wife is restricted from correcting her husband because in the process of her confronting him, he will have moments of discomfort from feeling inadequate. From his fear of humiliation, the wife is pushed into a docile position over the simplest conflicts. The result may be a very weak-willed woman who is afraid or unable to speak up for what she wants or what is right.

Esther combated this in King Ahasuerus. Her request for a banquet was not indecisive but a skillful political maneuver to overcome the first obstacle in saving her people from death. It was at the banquet that Esther finally revealed what her true intentions were. Even the setting of the banquet was part of a deliberate maneuver on Esther's part. The only people invited to the banquet were Haman and King Ahasuerus.

> "And that's not all," Haman added. "I'm the only person Queen Esther invited to accompany the king to the banquet she gave. And she has invited me along with the king tomorrow."
> —ESTHER 5:12

The isolated environment provided a safe place for Esther to speak to the king about a political issue, because without a large crowd, the king would be less likely to act upon his insecurity. The king also had a habit of consulting others to make decisions.

> Since it was customary for the king to consult experts in matters of law and justice, he spoke with the wise men who understood the times.
>
> —ESTHER 1:13

Although this was his habit, these counselors did not advise against the genocide intended for the Jewish people. Therefore, it can be speculated that Esther would need to isolate the king from his usual crowd of advisors.

When Esther accused Haman, the crowd could not be there to sway the opinion of the king. Also, the king would not be confronted with embarrassment for making such a terrible decision in appointing Haman as an official.

> So the king and Haman went to Queen Esther's banquet, and as they were drinking wine on the second day, the king again asked, "Queen Esther, what is your petition? It will be given you. What is your request? Even up to half the kingdom, it will be granted."
>
> Then Queen Esther answered, "If I have found favor with you, Your Majesty, and if it pleases you, grant me my life—this is my petition. And spare my people—this is my request. For I and my people have been sold to be destroyed, killed and annihilated. If we had merely been sold as male and female slaves, I would have kept quiet,

because no such distress would justify disturbing the king."

King Xerxes asked Queen Esther, "Who is he? Where is he—the man who has dared to do such a thing?"

Esther said, "An adversary and enemy! This vile Haman!"

Then Haman was terrified before the king and queen. The king got up in a rage, left his wine and went out into the palace garden. But Haman, realizing that the king had already decided his fate, stayed behind to beg Queen Esther for his life.

—ESTHER 7:1–7

King Ahasuerus left in a rage and went to the palace gardens. Rage is yet another irrational emotion the king could have easily been led by, but the strategic location of Esther's parley positioned the king to be alone to think rather than among the officials of Persia, who would think for him. When the king returned, he still didn't make a decision for himself, but one of his attendants made a suggestion and the king followed it:

Just as the king returned from the palace garden to the banquet hall, Haman was falling on the couch where Esther was reclining. The king exclaimed, "Will he even molest the queen while she is with me in the house?"

As soon as the word left the king's mouth, they covered Haman's face. Then Harbona, one of the eunuchs attending the king, said, "A pole reaching to a height of fifty cubits stands by Haman's house. He had it set up for Mordecai, who spoke up to help the king."

The king said, "Impale him on it!" So they impaled Haman on the pole he had set up for Mordecai. Then the king's fury subsided.

—ESTHER 7:8–10

Haman was hung on the gallows, but the problem did not end there. The issue of genocide had still not been addressed. Esther had to speak to the king again.

That same day King Xerxes gave Queen Esther the estate of Haman, the enemy of the Jews. And Mordecai came into the presence of the king, for Esther had told how he was related to her. The king took off his signet ring, which he had reclaimed from Haman, and presented it to Mordecai. And Esther appointed him over Haman's estate.

Esther again pleaded with the king, falling at his feet and weeping. She begged him to put an end to the evil plan of Haman the Agagite, which he had devised against the Jews.

—ESTHER 8:1–3

Esther had to overcome the brash thinking of the king while still unable to address the problem directly. The kingdom was set up so the king could not be confronted about bad decisions.

SAMPLE DIALOGUE:

"Ahasuerus, you hung Haman, but that still does not address the genocide that you agreed to against my people. You need to do something about Purim, the day that is designated for the destruction of my people."

The king responds, "I think I'm doing a great job as king. You always question every decision I make, and you don't even appreciate how I just gave you Haman's house and took care of the problem already. And I'm the master of this house; you don't tell me what to do."

The king looks at Esther condescendingly, then motions to have the guards take her away and behead her.

To the king, hanging Haman came across as simple logic and a solution to Esther's problem. *Haman bad. Hang Haman. Esther be happy now.* However, if the king's decision was really based on logic, he would be confronted with the fact that he chose Haman and agreed to his decision to commit genocide. The fact that Ahasuerus never addressed the decree to kill all the Jews showed that he did not think the problem through. Once more the king was protected from being seen as inadequate in problem solving, because the accountability of explaining the problem was placed upon the woman's indirect communication. He was clear of ever having been involved in the problem in the first place.

In relationships between husbands and wives, this is essentially called "playing dumb." The husband can fall back on "men just don't understand" when confronted about a lack of good judgment. Yet even in a state of supposedly misunderstanding his wife a husband still maintains his leadership position. If men are leaders then they should have the ability to understand simple issues such as the needs of their wives. If the man does not understand then he is a blind guide. Luke 6:39 says, "He also told them this parable: 'Can the blind lead the blind? Will they not both fall into a pit?'" So if a man is blind, he should not be leading, because he will drag his wife into a pit.

However, if he is not blind then his assumed logic-based decision-making process should be sound. Hanging Haman seemed logical, but logic would also lead to the conclusion that something would have to be done about the genocide decreed over the Jewish people. Yet King Ahasuerus did not come to that conclusion. Although he exuded logic, his decision-making process was very emotionally based. Every choice King Ahasuerus made was based on his fear of humiliation. Misuse of the biblical respect teaching functions in the same manner. A husband may make a choice that seems to be based on logic without thinking the problem through because his wife is indirect. He does not address the entire problem due to her indirectness, which is a result of his potential lashing out if she acted assertively—the root of the problem is his emotional fear of humiliation. The idea that women are solely emotional in making decisions is really a projection of the hidden emotional nature of men.

In the Book of Esther, the queen had to approach the king three times to address a time-sensitive issue. If Ahasuerus were truly logical he would have tried to find out the root of the problem at the first request. However, to do that, he would have to open himself to reproach, which would expose his emotional fear of humiliation.

When Esther spoke to Ahasuerus to finally address the genocide, she was crying. Esther's tears could have easily been mocked as the weak way in which women cope with stress and decision making. Ahasuerus had made many decisions during this time and had never cried about any of them. Based on the fact that Ahasuerus did not cry, maintaining the outwardly unemotional nature of men, some ascertain that men are more equipped for making hard choices. Yet the quality of choices and level of stress are not accounted for in that assumption.

From Ahasuerus's perspective, as the queen, Esther's life was relatively stress free. Her duties required only applying cosmetics, arraying herself as the queen, and pleasing him sexually when he was not occupied with the concubines or other things in his life. In truth, Esther had to face her death three times to ask her husband a question in an almost helpless situation to save her people from genocide. The only obstacle in King Ahasuerus's decision-making process was his fear of humiliation, which he had unlimited power to compensate for. There was also the religious political system of Persia, which enabled him to be viewed as a victim over the people he was victimizing.

As the king, Ahasuerus was in a coveted position of wealth and power. He often ran the risk of being used for gain. All the women in his harem could be faking the respect and attention they were giving him. If the king was perceived as a victim then he could be further justified in how he was treating the women in his life.

When the king was searching for a new queen to replace Vashti, he ordered that all the attractive virgins of the kingdom be gathered to the harem:

> Then the king's personal attendants proposed, "Let
> a search be made for beautiful young virgins for
> the king. Let the king appoint commissioners

in every province of his realm to bring all these beautiful young women into the harem at the citadel of Susa. Let them be placed under the care of Hegai, the king's eunuch, who is in charge of the women; and let beauty treatments be given to them. Then let the young woman who pleases the king be queen instead of Vashti." This advice appealed to the king, and he followed it.

—ESTHER 2:2–4

These women were never presented with a choice. Esther was taken into the harem.

When the king's order and edict had been proclaimed, many young women were brought to the citadel of Susa and put under the care of Hegai. Esther also was taken to the king's palace and entrusted to Hegai, who had charge of the harem.

—ESTHER 2:8

The word "taken" separates Esther from the women who assembled in the capital, but implies a forceful attendance. Then, the women were presented before the king:

Before a young woman's turn came to go in to King Xerxes, she had to complete twelve months of beauty treatments prescribed for the women, six months with oil of myrrh and six with perfumes and cosmetics. And this is how she would go to the king: Anything she wanted was given her to take with her from the harem to the king's palace. In the evening she would go there and in the morning return to another part of the harem to the care of Shaashgaz, the king's eunuch who was in charge of the concubines. She would not return to the king unless he was pleased with her and summoned her by name.

—Esther 2:12–14

The fact that the women were given nice things off- sets the fact that they were prisoners under guard of the king. Some were never given a choice before being taken to the harem, and they could never leave. Then, if the king did not call for a woman again, she would spend her life destitute in the harem. If a woman was brought before the king and did not conceive during her night with the king, and he did not remember her, she would remain in the harem childless, unable to approach the king for any request, with no opportu- nity to receive love from anyone else for the rest of her life, as she was still a wife of the king. To compensate for this type of cruel subjugation, the women could be portrayed as abusers of his title.

The perceived luxury of the harem offset the isolation and slavery of being a wife or concubine of the king. To create this luxury, the duties of women were restricted. It served a dual purpose of keeping them out of posi- tions of power so the men would have greater access to the women, and the comfort of the women's lives would counterbalance the sexual exploitation. As a woman of leisure, the queen would be further deterred from crit- icizing the king's decisions, further feeding into the system of him being inaccessible.

These same tactics are used today to discriminate against women in the workplace by limiting their economic resources to make them subject to a male influence. Also, women who choose to stay at home are met with skepticism when criticizing their husbands, because work at home is deemed a luxury compared to the duties of a man. If a woman does respond emotionally, her tears feed the stereotype that she is irrationally emotional for having an outburst over work that is deemed relatively easy, and the man is viewed as a victim of her manipulation. Husbands who ignore an emotional display from their wives can be further justified if they have tried to handle the problem in some way, even if their proposed solution was brash or incoherent.

Esther cried when facing the genocide of her people. King Ahasuerus had attempted to handle the problem by having Haman hanged, but his solution was not good enough. If the king was in a position of perpetual victimization, Esther's tears could just be manipulation. Her tears would also make him the victim of being told he was not good enough in the efforts he had already made. The belief system of Persia again aided in his potential to ignore a problem. Esther had to overcome barrier after barrier and still was forced to speak indirectly with the king, buttering him up with compliments before she finally asked for what she needed:

> Then the king extended the gold scepter to Esther and she arose and stood before him.
>
> "If it pleases the king," she said, "and if he regards me with favor and thinks it the right thing to do, and if he is pleased with me, let an order be written overruling the dispatches that Haman son of Hammedatha, the Agagite, devised and

wrote to destroy the Jews in all the king's provinces. For how can I bear to see disaster fall on my
people? How can I bear to see the destruction of
my family?"

—ESTHER 8:4–6

Then, after two banquets and several roundabout
conversations, the king finally addressed his decision to
condone genocide:

King Xerxes replied to Queen Esther and to
Mordecai the Jew, "Because Haman attacked the
Jews, I have given his estate to Esther, and they
have impaled him on the pole he set up. Now
write another decree in the king's name in behalf
of the Jews as seems best to you, and seal it with
the king's signet ring—for no document written in
the king's name and sealed with his ring can be
revoked."

—ESTHER 8:7–8

Then the king had to meet with his secretaries to
come to a solution:

At once the royal secretaries were summoned—
on the twenty-third day of the third month, the
month of Sivan. They wrote out all Mordecai's
orders to the Jews, and to the satraps, governors
and nobles of the 127 provinces stretching from
India to Cush. These orders were written in the
script of each province and the language of each
people and also to the Jews in their own script
and language. Mordecai wrote in the name of
King Xerxes, sealed the dispatches with the king's

signet ring, and sent them by mounted couriers, who rode fast horses especially bred for the king.

The king's edict granted the Jews in every city the right to assemble and protect themselves; to destroy, kill and annihilate the armed men of any nationality or province who might attack them and their women and children, and to plunder the property of their enemies. The day appointed for the Jews to do this in all the provinces of King Xerxes was the thirteenth day of the twelfth month, the month of Adar. A copy of the text of the edict was to be issued as law in every province and made known to the people of every nationality so that the Jews would be ready on that day to avenge themselves on their enemies.

—ESTHER 8:9–13

After this second decree was issued, the Jewish people were free to defend themselves against the ones who were trying to destroy them. Then, the king reported to Esther and asked her what to do.

The number of those killed in the citadel of Susa was reported to the king that same day. The king said to Queen Esther, "The Jews have killed and destroyed five hundred men and the ten sons of Haman in the citadel of Susa. What have they done in the rest of the king's provinces? Now what is your petition? It will be given you. What is your request? It will also be granted."

"If it pleases the king," Esther answered, "give the Jews in Susa permission to carry out this day's edict tomorrow also, and let Haman's ten sons be impaled on poles."

> So the king commanded that this be done. An
> edict was issued in Susa, and they impaled the ten
> sons of Haman.
>
> —ESTHER 9:11–14

When she gave the order to hang Haman's sons, Esther
was finally able to act as a military leader. Haman's sons
had already been killed; hanging them was an act to
show dominance and keep the Jewish army unified in
the war effort. Seeing the hanged bodies of Haman's
sons would give her people further hope in the cause as
news of victory would spread. It would also be seen as a
stern message to the adversaries of the Jews of the out-
come that awaited them. Using her strategic leadership,
Esther sent a message of hope while instilling fear into
the enemy.

Finishing Haman's sons was also in alignment with
God's plan to exact judgment on the Agagites; correcting
the failure of her predecessor Saul. Saul was from the
tribe of Benjamin from Israel. He was the first king of
Israel. When warring against the enemies of Israel, King
Saul was supposed to wipe out the enemy completely,
sparing no one. However, Saul was insubordinate in carrying out his orders, and kept the king alive and took
the forbidden spoils.

> But Saul and the army spared Agag and the best of
> the sheep and cattle, the fat calves[a] and lambs—
> everything that was good. These they were
> unwilling to destroy completely, but everything
> that was despised and weak they totally destroyed.
> —1 SAMUEL 15:9

Haman, an Agagite (a descendant of Agag), arose to take vengeance against the Jews because of Saul's failure to completely eliminate the enemy. Saul's style of half solving the problem when given a mission was akin to the system of Persia, where the king was not accountable for poor decisions. However, Esther, who was of the tribe of Benjamin, took on the mantle and accomplished the work God had instructed Israel to do. Executing Haman, then eliminating his seed, brought the work to completion.

Under the leadership of Saul as king of Israel, the army steadily drifted away from him because of his weakness in following through with his duty. Esther as queen unified the people in a public display of swift justice on the enemies of Israel. Once Esther was free from the bondages of a culturally instituted indirect communication, she proved to be a capable military leader.

After the victory of the Jewish people, there was a celebration. Even the celebration itself was a show of force to show that the security of the Jewish people was a product of the unified war effort.

> So Queen Esther, daughter of Abihail, along with Mordecai the Jew, wrote with full authority to confirm this second letter concerning Purim.
> —ESTHER 9:29

Esther led the army, and Mordecai served as her capable general. Then Esther made her own decree, giving the order to confirm the recognition of the victory.

> Esther's decree confirmed these regulations about
> Purim, and it was written down in the records.
>
> —ESTHER 9:32

The adversaries that Esther contended against were Haman, the religious and political system of Persia, and her husband, who was a product of the beliefs of the Persian Empire. These enemies still exist today in the form of assimilation of Persian culture into the Word of God. The legal system of Persia was contradictory and incoherent. Laws were in place, but they were disregarded and created at will. This is in direct contrast to God's laws, which are consistent and meant to be carried out without partiality.

The Diaspora occurred as God's disciplining His chosen people. However, the influence of Babylon, Media, and Persia was intended only as a temporary state. Not only was it temporary, but upon Israel's release from exile they were to judge the nations that took them captive for mistreating them. The Book of Daniel gives the allusion in reference to warring against Persia:

> So he said, "Do you know why I have come to you?
> Soon I will return to fight against the prince of
> Persia, and when I go, the prince of Greece will
> come."
>
> —DANIEL 10:20

The prince of Persia is one of the enemies of God, yet Persian practices continue to be embraced among His people. One in particular is the interaction between husbands and wives. The Persian view of marriage has been confused with the godly approach to marriage. The biblical commitment for a wife to respect her husband is applied to the Persian harem life of women, where respect is relegated to compliance in all matters, even if they are unjust and wicked.

Genocide is wrong. Remaining silent while someone seeks to commit genocide is wrong. Yet if the person enabling genocide is a husband, under the Persian view of marriage, the wife is expected to compromise with him. This same type of compromise has integrated itself into the body of believers. The issue may not be genocide, but rather than standing on God's Word, a woman is constantly placed in a position of compromise to appease her husband. This is the same way the Persian law would be set aside on the whims of the king. The integration of the two cultures is used by men to nullify the laws of God.

God's law says that He will judge anyone who curses Israel.

> The LORD had said to Abram, "Go from your country, your people and your father's household to the land I will show you.
> "I will make you into a great nation, and I will bless you; I will make your name great, and you will be a blessing. I will bless those who bless you, and whoever curses you I will curse; and all peoples on earth will be blessed through you."
> —GENESIS 12:1–3

Had Esther been silent, blindly compliant to her Persian husband, she would have brought a curse on herself by allowing Persia to curse the Jews. Esther risked her life and contended against not only Haman, but against the entire Persian Empire. She made the choice to break Persian law to uphold God's law.

> Then Esther sent this reply to Mordecai: "Go, gather together all the Jews who are in Susa, and fast for me. Do not eat or drink for three days, night or day. I and my attendants will fast as you do. When this is done, I will go to the king, even though it is against the law. And if I perish, I perish."
>
> —ESTHER 4:15–16

Esther was willing to lay down her own life in pursuit of righteousness. As soldiers in the army of God, women must understand that they are accountable to do what is correct, not to blindly follow a leader, even if that leader is your husband. They must understand that they are capable of making decisive choices and they have the right to contend against wicked people in authority.

Chapter 4

INSUBORDINATE SOLDIERS

SATAN IS AT war with God's kingdom. In his attempt to usurp the authority of God, he was thrown out of heaven.

> He replied, "I saw Satan fall like lightning from heaven."
>
> —LUKE 10:18

The details of Satan's rebellion are not revealed until the last book of the Bible. Revelation describes this conflict as a divine war.

> Then war broke out in heaven. Michael and his angels fought against the dragon, and the dragon and his angels fought back. But he was not strong enough, and they lost their place in heaven. The

great dragon was hurled down—that ancient serpent called the devil, or Satan [the Adversary],
who leads the whole world astray. He was hurled
to the earth, and his angels with him.

—REVELATION 12:7–9

After his fall, Satan landed on the earth. The Bible
begins with Genesis describing the creation of the earth
without referring to the backstory of why there was darkness on the land after heaven and earth were created.

In the beginning God created the heavens and the
earth. 2 Now the earth was formless and empty,
darkness was over the surface of the deep, and the
Spirit of God was hovering over the waters.

—GENESIS 1:1–2

God proceeded to divide the light from the darkness
and create the rest of the world.

Throughout Genesis chapter 1, God saw that everything He made was good. Since there is no darkness
in God, and His presence was abiding in creation, the
only resting place for Satan was the tree of knowledge
of good and evil. Humankind was created on the sixth
day, after the war in heaven, and was given the specific
instruction to subdue the earth and rule over every
living creature.

God blessed them and said to them, "Be fruitful
and increase in number; fill the earth and subdue
it. Rule over the fish in the sea and the birds in the
sky and over every living creature that moves on
the ground."

—GENESIS 1:28

The cause for the earth to be subdued would be to war against the darkness that resided at the tree of good and evil: Satan.

Adam was created as a solider to guard against the works of the evil one. Conversely, in an act of treason, Adam came into agreement with God's enemy and partook of good and evil. The punishment for this act, the fruits of his sin, was death. However, God in His mercy provided redemption from death through His Son, Yeshua, the Messiah.

> For God so loved the world that he gave his one and only Son, that whoever believes in him shall not perish but have eternal life.
> —JOHN 3:16

Before personal salvation is ever mentioned, though, the Scripture says that God loved the world. This shows how much God valued the earth itself. Since God gave dominion over the earth to humans, His Son came in the form of a human to act in the proper authority to save the world, while in the process saving the people that believe in him.

This means redemption is not intended solely for personal glory, but to destroy the works of the evil one.

> The one who does what is sinful is of the devil, because the devil has been sinning from the beginning. The reason the Son of God appeared was to destroy the devil's work.
> —1 JOHN 3:8

Satan has not given up in his attempts to steal the kingdom of God away.

> From the days of John the Baptist until now, the kingdom of heaven has been subjected to violence, and violent people have been raiding it.
>
> —MATTHEW 11:12

Yet the body of believers continues in the failure of Adam by agreeing with teachings of the enemy, then blaming others, particularly women, for failing in their duties to stand against God's enemies.

Believers fail to be good stewards over the land and convict sin. There is a deep connection between the authority humans carry over the earth and the land itself. When people sin, the results are a negative reaction from the land. God warned the people of Israel that the land itself would vomit them out for not keeping His laws.

> But you must keep my decrees and my laws. The native-born and the foreigners residing among you must not do any of these detestable things, for all these things were done by the people who lived in the land before you, and the land became defiled. And if you defile the land, it will vomit you out as it vomited out the nations that were before you.
>
> —LEVITICUS 18:26–28

The prophet Jeremiah said that the laws of nature were overturned because of sin: "Your crimes have overturned nature's rules, your sins have kept back good from you" (Jer. 5:25, CJB). This is why there is increased intensity behind natural disasters when people sin. Even Paul describes the earth as groaning over the sin present upon it: "We know that the whole creation has been groaning as in the pains of childbirth right up to the present time" (Rom. 8:22). It is important for people to stop sinning and enforce the laws of God for more than personal growth, but because Adam's requirement to subdue the land is a standing order. Believers are redeemed for God, by Yeshua, for the purpose of fulfilling the duty Adam failed to uphold.

The only tool Satan has in his war against God is deception. Satan has crafted his hypocrisy in religious theology to deceive the masses into tolerating sin. Theologies teach the unconditional forgiveness of sin. Scriptures that talk about how all things can be forgiven are used to justify an obligation to forgive at all costs. This elaborate deception includes a mixture of the truth from the Scripture as well as the lie. The Scripture says to forgive, but the lie is that there are no conditions or expectations to obtain forgiveness.

> So watch yourselves. "If your brother or sister sins against you, rebuke them; and if they repent, forgive them."
>
> —LUKE 17:3

When Yeshua said this, He outlined a clear pattern for forgiveness. First, the person who sinned must be rebuked. Then, "if" he repents, forgive him. Satan's hypocrisy in theology forces people to move straight to forgiveness without ever correcting the one who sinned. As a result, evildoers and sinners are embraced with love rather than being held accountable. Sinners are never confronted with the consequences of their actions and are then emboldened to continue sinning.

> For certain men whose condemnation was written about long ago have secretly slipped in among you. They are godless men, who change the grace of our God into a license for immorality and deny Yeshua the Messiah our only Sovereign and Lord.
> —JUDE 4, NCPE

With sin taking a stronghold, the land becomes defiled under its inhabitants, and for the sake of forgiveness the body of believers does not confront sin, forsaking their authority over the land.

The land is important because as soldiers in the army of God, believers are supposed to gain territory for His kingdom. The ultimate plan of God is to manifest physically and dwell among His people.

> But I will walk among you and be your God, and you will be my people.
> —LEVITICUS 26:12

God lived with His creation in the Garden of Eden before Adam allowed sin to breach. After sin defiled humanity, a physical distance was created between humanity and God, because God cannot dwell in a place where there is defilement. Yeshua the Messiah cleansed humanity from sin so humanity can be reunited with God.

> And put everything under his feet. In putting everything under him, God left nothing that is not

subject to him. Yet at present we do not see everything subject to him.

—HEBREWS 2:8, NCPE

Because everything is subject to Yeshua, everything is cleaned, but it is not seen in its fullness, because coming under subjection to Yeshua is a process of applying the cleansing of the blood of the Messiah, from a spiritual cleaning to a physical cleaning. Meanwhile, during that process, Satan actively wars against this restoration coming to the physical realm. Satan's plan is to defile all the land to prevent God from physically inhabiting His kingdom. To gain access to the land to defile it, Satan has to go through humankind, which was given dominion over the land.

> Truly I tell you, whatever you bind on earth will be bound in heaven, and whatever you loose on earth will be loosed in heaven.
>
> —MATTHEW 18:18

Therefore, if sin is allowed on earth, then sin will be permitted in heaven, preventing God from ruling. The converse is true as well—if sin is prohibited on earth, it will be prohibited in heaven, bringing forth God's rule on earth as it is in heaven. When Yeshua said this to His disciples, it was in reference to taking authority over sin in the physical realm and how it affects the spiritual, and vice versa. If believers remain under the theology of unconditional forgiveness, overlooking rebuking the sinners and the responsibility of the sinner to repent, sin is then permitted on earth, physically blocking the kingdom of God.

Exclusively focusing on the spiritual aspects of God limits His manifestations in the physical. The physical state of righteousness is how the law of God is applied to life. For example, spiritual fornication is sexual immorality in the form of fantasy, whereas physical fornication is acting upon any given sexual immorality. Both are sins and inhibit God from dwelling with His people. Shifting all the focus to the spiritual is another deception from the enemy to trivialize the importance of the physical. If the physical were not important, then Satan would never attack people in their physical circumstances.

Sin is a physical defilement of the land. The blood of Yeshua purifies the land and the people from defilement, but the forgiveness that the blood of Yeshua offers is not to be used as an excuse to keep sinning. Persistent sinning after receiving grace invalidates the grace that Messiah offers.

> It is impossible for those who have once been enlightened, who have tasted the heavenly gift, who have shared in the Holy Spirit, who have tasted the goodness of the word of God and the powers of the coming age and who have fallen away, to be brought back to repentance. To their loss they are crucifying the Son of God all over again and subjecting him to public disgrace. Land that drinks in the rain often falling on it and that produces a crop useful to those for whom it is farmed receives the blessing of God. But land that produces thorns and thistles is worthless and is in danger of being cursed. In the end it will be burned.
>
> —HEBREWS 6:4–8

The unconditional forgiveness theology is a carefully crafted deception to get believers to treat the forgiveness that the blood of Yeshua offers as common and thereby bring the land under a curse. Unconditional forgiveness is a cycle of sin and absolution where Yeshua is crucified over and over without the guilty party repenting. While this cycle repeats, the one being sinned against also falls in derision at the hands of an unrepentant sinner. For instance, someone who has been wronged could be held in contempt for unforgiveness for seeking justice while the guilty party is exonerated by false grace that deems the one offended is obligated to forgive. The unconditional forgiveness theology promotes victim blaming.

When Yeshua sent His disciples out into the world, He instructed them about forgiving and holding sins.

> Again Yeshua said, "Peace be with you! As the Father has sent me, I am sending you." And with that he breathed on them and said, "Receive the Holy Spirit." If you forgive anyone his sins, they are forgiven; if you do not forgive them, they are not forgiven.
> —JOHN 20:21–23, NCPE

The disciples were given instructions on holding sins as well as forgiving them, because there would be clear instances where sin had to be held for the accountability of the guilty party. What is taught in the body of believers is that no sins are to be held on account of salvation. This perversion is taught so pervasively that the body of believers fails to expel the wicked from among them.

God will judge those outside. "Expel the wicked
person from among you."

—1 Corinthians 5:13

Under unconditional forgiveness evildoers are not
identified and continue to function within the body.
Then, believers act on the exact opposite of what they
are supposed to do and attempt to judge nonbelievers.
As a result, the body of believers becomes a safe haven
for hypocrites while victims are trampled upon. The
body spends its time attempting to judge outsiders while
ignoring the people within who create divisions.

One example of this perversion and its devastating
results took place during the time of David, King of
Israel. As the king, David was responsible for enforcing
the law of God. This is contrary to the kings of secular
monarchies, who decreed, wrote, and created their own
laws. Each anointed king of Israel was responsible for
keeping his own copy of the law and judging based only
on God's Word.

When he takes the throne of his kingdom, he is
to write for himself on a scroll a copy of this law,
taken from that of the Levitical priests.

—Deuteronomy 17:18

This is similar to the way God told Adam to subdue
and guard the Garden of Eden.

Late into his kingship, David sinned with adultery
and murder, which opened the door for sin to enter into
his family and the entire kingdom. After David sinned,
a curse came over him that the sword would never leave
his house and evil would come against him from his

own household. This is similar to the way Adam sinned, and sin, by means of death, affects all human beings.

After David sinned, his son, Amnon, became fixated on his half-sister Tamar. He pretended to be sick so David would send Tamar to help him. Then, when Tamar came to help him, he raped her.

> Then she took the pan and served him the bread, but he refused to eat.
>
> "Send everyone out of here," Amnon said. So everyone left him. Then Amnon said to Tamar, "Bring the food here into my bedroom so I may eat from your hand." And Tamar took the bread she had prepared and brought it to her brother Amnon in his bedroom. But when she took it to him to eat, he grabbed her and said, "Come to bed with me, my sister."
>
> "No, my brother!" she said to him. "Don't force me! Such a thing should not be done in Israel! Don't do this wicked thing. What about me? Where could I get rid of my disgrace? And what about you? You would be like one of the wicked fools in Israel. Please speak to the king; he will not keep me from being married to you." But he refused to listen to her, and since he was stronger than she, he raped her.
>
> Then Amnon hated her with intense hatred. In fact, he hated her more than he had loved her. Amnon said to her, "Get up and get out!"
>
> "No!" she said to him. "Sending me away would be a greater wrong than what you have already done to me."
>
> But he refused to listen to her. He called his personal servant and said, "Get this woman out of

> my sight and bolt the door after her." So his servant put her out and bolted the door after her. She was wearing an ornate robe, for this was the kind of garment the virgin daughters of the king wore. Tamar put ashes on her head and tore the ornate robe she was wearing. She put her hands on her head and went away, weeping aloud as she went.
>
> —2 SAMUEL 13:9–19

After hearing about this, David was angry but did not act.

> When King David heard all this, he was furious.
>
> —2 SAMUEL 13:21

In accordance to the law, Amnon deserved death.

> "Cursed is anyone who sleeps with his sister, the daughter of his father or the daughter of his mother." Then all the people shall say, "Amen!"
>
> —DEUTERONOMY 27:22

Amnon's behavior was tolerated because he was David's son. The Septuagint adds in its account of this story, "but he (David) did not rebuke his son Amnon, for he favored him, since he was his first-born." This sent two messages that were contrary to God.

The first message is that the son of a king has the right to commit crimes and go unpunished. The second message is that a son is given preference to a daughter, because given the choice, the king chose to absolve his son rather than defend his daughter. This message continues today when someone can confess Yeshua—which makes them a king's son—and then be exonerated from the guilt of their sin against another person; particularly if that person whom they sinned against is a woman. The presumed "king's son" is also forgiven without question under the unconditional forgiveness theology.

God clearly commands that the guilty should not be exonerated:

> Do not pervert justice or show partiality. Do not accept a bribe, for a bribe blinds the eyes of the wise and twists the words of the innocent. Follow justice and justice alone, so that you may live and possess the land the LORD your God is giving you.
> —DEUTERONOMY 16:19–20

Two years later, David's other son Absalom invited Amnon to a sheep-shearing festival and had Amnon killed. This means that for two years Amnon was living out his life without rebuke or punishment. It was a known fact that Amnon was a rapist. The first people to become aware of his perversions would have been his servants.

When Amnon set up the circumstances to be alone with Tamar, he had ordered all the servants to leave him. However, after he raped her, he called his personal servant. Therefore, it can be speculated that when Amnon told the servants to leave, it meant only to leave the room. They were probably close by to hear him call for their return at a moment's notice.

The servant took Tamar, put her out, and locked the door behind her as Amnon requested. The scripture says that Amnon had overpowered her to rape her, which implies that he did not simply use intimidation but physical force. So there were likely to be visible signs of forcible rape such as bruises and blood. She had a long-sleeved robe, but her appearance was probably disheveled. Also with the assumption that the servants were still waiting close by after Amnon sent them out, they may have heard her screaming or the brief dialogue that went on between Tamar and Amnon.

The servant who put her out was a witness to the wrong that had been done to her. Yet with all this potential evidence available, the servant did not hesitate to carry out Amnon's orders. The servant's actions showed a blind obedience to authority even if ordered to do something wrong. Since Amnon was a king's son, carrying with him the authority and privileges that came with that, the servant was now willfully involved in transgression.

This is also a problem today, where scriptures about respecting authority are used to create blind compliance. References to believers being like soldiers further reinforces the importance of submission to authority. However, what is often omitted is that soldiers and servants are only supposed to obey legal orders.

> Do not follow the crowd in doing wrong. When
> you give testimony in a lawsuit, do not pervert jus-
> tice by siding with the crowd.
>
> —EXODUS 23:2

Not following the crowd may include defying someone in a high position. In following only legal orders, believers have a responsibility to resist any authority that tries to issue an illegal order. For example, when Saul was king, in a jealous fury he wanted to kill David.

When David fled from him, Saul wanted to kill anyone who had helped him, so he ordered his men to kill even the priests of God.

> Then the king ordered the guards at his side: "Turn and kill the priests of the LORD, because they too have sided with David. They knew he was fleeing, yet they did not tell me."
> But the king's officials were unwilling to raise a hand to strike the priests of the LORD.
> —1 SAMUEL 22:17

Had Saul's men obeyed this illegal order, they would have been under condemnation for killing the priest of God. Saul was the Lord's anointed, yet his anointing from God did not trump God's law.

> Those who guide this people mislead them, and those who are guided are led astray.
> —ISAIAH 9:16

Following a leader in evil is no excuse. God does not destroy people unjustly or without cause, so allowing oneself to be led by a wicked leader is a sin. Every believer has the responsibility to uphold God's Word in the grand scheme of the divine war that is taking place. Yet many have become insubordinate to the cause on account of a leader telling them to do something that is openly against God.

Another example of having to defy a leader who gave an illegal order is the story of the Egyptian midwives:

> The king of Egypt said to the Hebrew midwives, whose names were Shiphrah and Puah, "When

you are helping the Hebrew women during childbirth on the delivery stool, if you see that the baby
is a boy, kill him; but if it is a girl, let her live."
The midwives, however, feared God and did not
do what the king of Egypt had told them to do;
they let the boys live. Then the king of Egypt summoned the midwives and asked them, "Why have
you done this? Why have you let the boys live?"

The midwives answered Pharaoh, "Hebrew
women are not like Egyptian women; they are vig-
orous and give birth before the midwives arrive."

So God was kind to the midwives and the people
increased and became even more numerous. And
because the midwives feared God, he gave them
families of their own.

—Exodus 1:15–21

There is no authority that God did not place, so
Pharaoh was raised up by God's authority. However,
when Pharaoh made an illegal order, the Egyptian midwives refused to follow it. Then God blessed them for
defying and lying to Pharaoh.

Amnon's servant, on the other hand, aided in the evil
Amnon committed without question because Amnon
was the king's son. Accountability for right and wrong
were removed by claiming that a servant was never
given a choice to decipher the truth.

This type of thinking is present in the body of
believers today. The results are people taking on the
traits of infallibility because they are the king's sons—
by way of confessing Yeshua. Then those who become
infallible under the "king's son clause" lead or follow
in unquestioning compliance to authority. The law of

God is no longer applied to any given situation but is secondary to unconditional forgiveness of the king's sons and following the orders of the religious authority at all costs, even if sin is the consequence of their compliance.

As members of the army of God, all believers fall into dissention. In response, there are those who throw off all authority upon becoming aware of the hypocrisy of the religious system.

> The wise in heart accept commands, but a chattering fool comes to ruin.
>
> —PROVERBS 10:8

On the other side, the religious system is in a continual battle with the outsiders who point out the faults of the believers, while the believers refuse to correct the evil within their own camp. Then Satan can easily continue to reign with the people doing all the work for him in destroying each other. This same battle format appeared when Absalom staged a coup against his father, David.

For two years Amnon lived without any culpability for raping Tamar. His guilt affected not only his victim, but it became a bitter root that affected others as well. First, the servants and all others who were aware of Amnon's crime came under guilt for not reporting what had happened to Tamar.

> If anyone sins because they do not speak up when they hear a public charge to testify regarding

something they have seen or learned about, they will be held responsible.

—LEVITICUS 5:1

Then, Absalom was embittered.

And Absalom never said a word to Amnon, either good or bad; he hated Amnon because he had disgraced his sister Tamar.

—2 SAMUEL 13:22

When Yeshua instructed His followers to rebuke someone for sinning, He was actually referencing what had been written in the Law. The Scripture says that rather than secretly being angry, people are to rebuke sin.

Do not hate a fellow Israelite in your heart. Rebuke your neighbor frankly so you will not share in their guilt.

—LEVITICUS 19:17

Absalom sinned in harboring this hatred for his brother. Everyone who did not rebuke Amnon was guilty.

Next, Amnon's sin multiplied to involve Absalom and his servants. Absalom, in premeditation, invited his brother Amnon to a sheep-shearing festival in Baalhazor. Then he ordered his servants to slay Amnon when he was in high spirits from the wine. After Absalom had Amnon killed, he fled to Geshur.

Absalom was justified in having Amnon killed because the law says that a man who has relations with his sister should be put to death. However, Absalom was not authorized to carry out the sentence. King

David was responsible for enforcing the law, but he did not do it.

Absalom represents people who recognize the hypocrisy within the church and stray away as a result. Although it would have been tragic, David was obligated to have his son, Amnon, stoned to death. Because he did not do that, the bitter root expanded to involve several other people in sin. This is exactly Satan's plan to destroy humanity. Humanity is intended to war against Satan's principalities and rulers in high places. However, if humanity is involved in sin, they will be unfit to serve in God's army. Satan uses the bitter roots to contaminate many in order to break the ranks of the people in God's army.

God warns the people to expel the evildoer from among them—not because of wrath, but because one evildoer will destroy many.

> Make sure there is no man or woman, clan or tribe among you today whose heart turns away from the LORD our God to go and worship the gods of those nations; make sure there is no root among you that produces such bitter poison.
> —DEUTERONOMY 29:18

> See to it that no one falls short of the grace of God and that no bitter root grows up to cause trouble and defile many.
> —HEBREWS 12:15

First, the victim, Tamar, was contaminated by Amnon's sin. She remained desolate in Absalom's house after she was raped. The phrase "remaining desolate" implies that she was in a depressed, isolated, and hopeless state. Since her virginity had been stolen from her, she faced despair over her opportunity to ever have a husband. The inheritance of a woman was based upon being a joint heir with her husband, providing children to pass the inheritance to the next generation. So Amnon not only raped her but also stole her inheritance from her. Since he took Tamar's ability to obtain a husband, Amnon also cut off her family line from going forth. Then, if she had conceived as a result of incest, her child would be a bastard, *mamzer,* cursed and separated from God for ten generations.

Tamar likely had feelings of shame and guilt because of the violent crime that was committed against her. The isolation could have also been a symptom of estrangement from her father and everyone else that appeared indifferent to her cause, letting Amnon go unpunished.

Next, everyone with knowledge of the crime who did not speak up came under guilt. Then, Absalom and his servants were the next level of contamination from the bitter root. After Absalom had Amnon killed, he fled to Geshur and lived there for three years.

The fact that Absalom picked Geshur as a place of refuge was not random. He was royalty on both sides of his family because his mother was the daughter of the king of Geshur.

> Sons were born to David in Hebron: His firstborn was Amnon the son of Ahinoam of Jezreel; his second, Kileab the son of Abigail the widow

of Nabal of Carmel; the third, Absalom the son of
Maakah daughter of Talmai king of Geshur.

—2 SAMUEL 3:2–3

Geshur was a kingdom that inhabited land within
Israel. The Israelites were supposed to have eliminated
that kingdom during the time of Joshua but did not
follow God's order.

> However the people of Israel expelled neither the
> Geshurites not the Maachathites, with the con-
> sequence that Geshurites and Maachathites have
> lived among Israel to this day.
>
> —JOSHUA 13:13

The inhabitants who were left in Israel then became a
snare to the people.

> The angel of the LORD went up from Gilgal to
> Bokim and said, "I brought you up out of Egypt
> and led you into the land I swore to give to your
> ancestors. I said, 'I will never break my covenant
> with you, and you shall not make a covenant with
> the people of this land, but you shall break down
> their altars.' Yet you have disobeyed me. Why
> have you done this? And I have also said, 'I will
> not drive them out before you; they will become
> traps for you, and their gods will become snares
> to you.'"
>
> —JUDGES 2:1–3

For the three years Absalom spent in Geshur with
the other side of his family, it could be speculated that
the Geshurites had influence over him. Even if he had

never returned to Israel, Absalom would have still been in a position of power and potential kingship, being the grandson of the king of Geshur by way of his mother. With the curse of leaving the inhabitants in the land becoming a snare, it can also be speculated that the king of Geshur would want to seek revenge against the king of Israel, David, for past conquest. Absalom, who clearly resented his family on account of what was done to his sister, would then be the perfect vessel for manipulation against David. So, Absalom would be under the influence of the idolatry of Geshur as well as animosity toward Israel.

Now, the bitter root had further expanded to include the enemies of God and His people. This is similar to someone who leaves the body of believers because of the hypocrisy and then becomes involved in other religions. False religions are critical of God's Word. By fault finding and making accusations, these false doctrines seek to usurp God's authority in the same manner Satan tries to usurp God's authority. The person who falls into the trap of false doctrine comes into agreement with Satan, because Satan accuses the brethren before God daily.

After Absalom returned from Israel, he staged a coup against his father. To do this, he first won over the hearts of the people.

> In the course of time, Absalom provided himself with a chariot and horses and with fifty men to run ahead of him. He would get up early and stand by the side of the road leading to the city gate. Whenever anyone came with a complaint to be placed before the king for a decision, Absalom

would call out to him, "What town are you from?" He would answer, "Your servant is from one of the tribes of Israel." Then Absalom would say to him, "Look, your claims are valid and proper, but there is no representative of the king to hear you." And Absalom would add, "If only I were appointed judge in the land! Then everyone who has a complaint or case could come to me and I would see that they receive justice."

—2 SAMUEL 15:1–4

The people who were seeking the king were going for judgments, meaning they were already in a state of lack in some area of their lives. As they were on their way to the king, Absalom would intercept them. Then Absalom would underhandedly criticize the king. When he would tell the person he was speaking to, "If only I were appointed judge in the land...," he was implying, "I would have done something by now."

It was common knowledge in Israel what Amnon had done to Tamar, and how David the king never sought justice over that issue. On the other hand, Absalom sought justice on behalf of his sister. Now, when he was talking to the people, he could win their hearts by subtly reminding them of David's shortcomings, thus planting the idea that if Absalom was king instead, he would do better.

This is exactly how Satan deceived Eve. Under the weak leadership of Adam, who did not confront the snake when the lie was first introduced, Satan could plant the idea in her head that eating the forbidden fruit was acceptable.

After Absalom won the hearts of the people, he proclaimed himself king of Israel. Just like in the Garden of Eden, after sin manifested physically with the forbidden fruit being eaten, Satan took authority as prince of the air.

> In which you used to live when you followed the ways of this world and of the ruler of the kingdom of the air, the spirit who is now at work in those who are disobedient.
> —EPHESIANS 2:2

After Absalom usurped authority, proclaiming himself king, the bitter root continued to expand to those who were led astray by a false king, like people led astray by Satan's lies. David fled from Jerusalem, and Israel was split by war.

> David's army marched out of the city to fight Israel, and the battle took place in the forest of Ephraim. There Israel's troops were routed by David's men, and the casualties that day were great—twenty thousand men. The battle spread out over the whole countryside, and the forest swallowed up more men that day than the sword.
> —2 SAMUEL 18:6–8

Once again the bitter root expanded. Now it included twenty thousand people, because the sin of Amnon was not judged properly.

The battle can represent the battle between believers within the church and unbelievers. There is a distinct group of people who are led astray because of the hypocrisy of the church for harboring the wicked. This group allies themselves with a false king. Then there are David's servants, who follow the correct king but still experience the devastation of fighting within their own kingdom. The battle itself is the true loss, because although David's servants won, there were significant losses on both sides, with the terrain destroying more people than the sword. The battle also was a distraction. Since Israel was in a civil war, they were not fighting their real enemies and Satan.

This is exactly how Satan functions. Satan has no power, and the only tool he has is to elicit deception to get people to war against God for him. It began with David failing to uphold the law of God by committing adultery and murder, opening the door for sin, the same way Adam did. Next, a bitter root was established because Amnon was not judged for his sin when he raped Tamar. Then, the rest of the house of Israel was contaminated with sin and death after a coup and civil war. As a result, over twenty thousand people were killed. Satan, who only wants destruction, was the true victor in claiming many lives from just one person failing to uphold one commandment to expel the evildoer from among the camp.

There was even further dissention within David's camp during this war, coming from the commanders.

> The king commanded Joab, Abishai and Ittai, "Be gentle with the young man Absalom for my sake." And all the troops heard the king giving orders concerning Absalom to each of the commanders.
> —2 Samuel 18:5

However, when Joab encountered Absalom, he deliberately disobeyed the king's order and killed him.

> Now Absalom happened to meet David's men. He was riding his mule, and as the mule went under the thick branches of a large oak, Absalom's hair got caught in the tree. He was left hanging in midair, while the mule he was riding kept on going.
> When one of the men saw what had happened, he told Joab, "I just saw Absalom hanging in an oak tree."
> Joab said to the man who had told him this, "What! You saw him? Why didn't you strike him to the ground right there? Then I would have had to give you ten shekels of silver and a warrior's belt."
> But the man replied, "Even if a thousand shekels were weighed out into my hands, I would not lay a hand on the king's son. In our hearing the king commanded you and Abishai and Ittai, 'Protect the young man Absalom for my sake.' And if I had put my life in jeopardy—and nothing is hidden from the king—you would have kept your distance from me."
> Joab said, "I'm not going to wait like this for you." So he took three javelins in his hand and plunged them into Absalom's heart while Absalom was still alive in the oak tree. And ten of Joab's armor-bearers surrounded Absalom, struck him and killed him.
>
> —2 SAMUEL 18:9–15

Militarily, killing Absalom may have been the better choice; however, it was still an act of defiance. The king, who was emotionally compromised, was open to be undermined by the people he was leading. Joab felt justified in disobeying orders, in the name of his own opinion.

This relates to the hundreds of denominations within the body of believers. They all claim to be serving the king, but they are not unified in obeying the king. Different denominations cherry-pick what scriptures they will follow or disregard the same way Joab did, based on the presiding conflict of misaligned leaders.

The hypocrisy and dissention also further estranges people who have been wronged. Joab had no problem acting on his own accord against the king, yet when Absalom acted on his own accord to vindicate his sister, he had to go into exile. Joab also was obedient in carrying out the first illegal order from David, sending Uriah to the front line and drawing back so he would be murdered. So the kingdom again sent the message that mutiny was acceptable for personal decisions, but acting on behalf of a woman who had been violated and her inheritance stolen was insignificant. Joab made himself to be a judge of the king, but he did not have the wherewithal to make a judgment to do the right thing on behalf of Tamar, or when David's illegal order was issued.

Amnon received unconditional forgiveness for rape, because nothing was done to him. The bitter root from his sin sparked a civil war in Israel. The death as a result of this war defiled the land. The leadership of Israel was thrown into confusion. Lines between obedience and standing for what was right became blurred. The authority of leaders chosen by God is supposed to be honored, but when the leaders are wrong, the people under them are left to a no-win situation. The people can do what is right, but at the cost of dishonoring authority. Then others, seeing that doing what is right comes at the cost of disregarding authority, become emboldened to outright rebel, whether or not their cause is correct. This blurs the lines between obedience and righteousness, and between who is on the outside for justice and who is on the outside because of wickedness.

This is the state of the body of believers today, where unconditional forgiveness creates bitter roots among the people. Divisions among believers arise because of cherry-picking scriptures, when the judgment that is required for sin is misdirected. To correct this, Yeshua's example of how to judge must be followed.

> Do not judge, or you too will be judged. For in the same way you judge others, you will be judged, and with the measure you use, it will be measured to you.
>
> Why do you look at the speck of sawdust in your brother's eye and pay no attention to the plank in your own eye? How can you say to your brother, "Let me take the speck out of your eye," when all the time there is a plank in your own eye? You hypocrite, first take the plank out of your own eye, and then you will see clearly to remove the speck from your brother's eye.
>
> —MATTHEW 7:1–5

On the surface it would appear that Yeshua was saying that we should not judge at all. But in verse 5 He said, "You hypocrite, first take the plank out of your own eye." He was giving a step-by-step process. First, one's own actions have to be corrected. Continuing in verse

5, Yeshua said, "then you will see clearly to remove the speck from your brother's eye." After owning up and repenting of your own sins, you are commanded to remove the splinter from your brother's eye. Following Yeshua's instruction on this requires a change in behavior on the part of the self first, and then influencing others to change.

Joab is an example of someone judging while having a pole in their eye. Joab had a history of disobeying the king's orders. He made an unauthorized kill during the time of peace to avenge his brother when he killed Abner in 2 Samuel chapter 3. Had Joab been righteous, he would have considered his own shortcomings before deliberately disobeying the king. Joab was silent in judging Amnon by inaction, but then he tried to get the splinter out of Absalom's eye, someone who had also made an unauthorized kill to avenge a sibling. Joab was an insubordinate solider and a contributor to a civil war that defiled the land and aided in the plans of Satan to divide Israel.

Joab's hypocrisy made him incompetent in combating sin at its root.

> Stop judging by mere appearances, but instead judge correctly.
>
> —JOHN 7:24

Joab followed the pattern of Adam and allowed the land to come under a curse. Adam's first duty was to subdue the land. When Adam failed in his mission, he blamed Eve. Before Adam could justifiably confront Eve about what she had done wrong in presenting him with the forbidden fruit—the splinter in her eye—Adam should have addressed the pole in his eye, in that he did not subdue the land. His inaction when the snake first introduced his heresy to Eve is the same inaction used when no one—Joab or anyone else in Israel—judged Amnon for raping Tamar.

When Adam sinned, the ground became cursed on his account. The subsequent generations separated from God and fought against each other, just like Absalom's coup. In creating their own cultures and purposes, the generations after Adam became further estranged from their duty to subdue the land and they lost sight of who the true enemy is: Satan. God called Israel as His chosen people and gave them His law to realign humanity with its original purpose. Then, God sent His Son so that all of humanity could be reestablished in the army of God.

> But now in Messiah Yeshua you who once were far away have been brought near through the blood of Messiah...
>
> Consequently, you are no longer foreigners and aliens, but fellow citizens with God's people and members of God's household.
>
> —EPHESIANS 2:13, 19, NCPE

After one is reconciled to God, there stands the task of subduing the land. To subdue the land is to keep it free from the defilement of sin. To do that, believers must take a stand and judge properly. They must not allow forgiveness to be a conduit for accepting sin and harboring wickedness. Everyone must search their own ways and correct their faults based on God's standards. Then, evildoers—people who claim to follow God but remain unrepentant in their sins—must be removed from the body. When hypocrisy and bitter roots are removed, believers will stand unified as ready soldiers in God's army.

Chapter 5

COVENANT OF RAPE

APE IS A violent act of control and domination. Culturally, sexual violence is expected and trivialized because the psychological effects of sexual violence are intentionally used to subjugate all women. Rape becomes a covenant by a process of defiling marriage, cheating, or denying women an inheritance, and compromising God's Word through tolerance and justifying deviant behavior. When we come into a covenant of rape, the Word of God becomes nullified and compatible with false religions. The Bible includes many accounts where women are raped and brutalized, and the acceptance of that form of violence leads to the overall degradation of an entire people and further separation between God and man.

In biblical law a father is responsible for providing a home, food, and clothing for his daughter for her entire life or until she gets married. For a daughter to enter into marriage, her father releases her from his protection into a covenant of provision and protection with her husband. A covenant is a binding agreement made by two or more individuals to do, or keep from doing, a specified thing. When a father fails to defend his daughter, the effects are more than just neglect; he is actually releasing her into a covenant where she has to fend for herself. Vulnerable and exposed, she is left open to attack and curses. Repeated lack of action on the part of fathers to defend their daughters allows violence against women to become a cultural norm and a replacement for godly covenants.

The Book of Judges in the Bible contains many examples of fathers who failed to defend their daughters, subjecting them to brutal violence, and a cultural tolerance for those behaviors.

> In those days Israel had no king; everyone did as they saw fit.
>
> —JUDGES 21:25

When a man is only doing what he thinks is right, he can cherry-pick from God's Word the parts that benefit him while ignoring his responsibilities. Judges chapters 19–21 detail a brutal rape, a war within the tribes of Israel, generational iniquity, condoning the behavior of known rapists, and rash vows that led to more sexual violence against women.

In those days Israel had no king. Now a Levite
who lived in a remote area in the hill country of
Ephraim took a concubine from Bethlehem in
Judah. But she was unfaithful to him. She left him
and went back to her parents' home in Bethlehem,
Judah. After she had been there four months.

—Judges 19:1–2

The woman this Levite was with was a concubine,
not a wife. A concubine acts in the same way a wife
does, but there is no covenant binding the two in
any official obligations to one another. This is similar
to having a girlfriend as opposed to a wife. She was
unfaithful to him, but this Levite could not formally
make an adultery charge against her because the law
only applies to a wife.

Numbers 5:11–31 describes the law concerning a
husband who suspects that his wife has committed
adultery when there are no witnesses to bring a charge
against her. She was to be brought before the temple
of God, profess her innocence, and drink bitter water.
If she was guilty of committing adultery, her womb
would rot and she would become a curse. If she was
innocent, she would have children. This law protected women against frivolous charges of adultery and
jealous husbands, and was a monitor for the purity of a
marriage. But it could only be enacted for a legal wife,
not a concubine.

In the first two verses of Judges chapter 19, it is
revealed that the woman had not been officially released
into a covenant by her father. Although concubines
are mentioned throughout the Bible, they are never

condoned by God, and no allowances are made for them in the law. The system of concubines, where a man has permission to sleep with a woman who is not his wife, is purely man-made. It would not be in place if a father had intervened and saw to it that his daughter was not treated like a sex possession.

Taking concubines was so common that it created a lot of confusion about what it really was—fornication. Giving this fornication a different name blurred the lines between the truth and the lie. The concubine system was designed to be similar to a marriage to make it seem as though it was done under the authority of God; that way, women would be much less likely to combat it. Permitting fornication is one of the first steps to condoning sexual violence, because it nullifies the Word of God concerning sex within marriage, making sex common rather than holy.

> He replied, "Isaiah was right when he prophe-
> sied about you hypocrites; as it is written: 'These
> people honor me with their lips, but their hearts
> are far from me. They worship me in vain; their
> teachings are merely human rules.' You have let
> go of the commands of God and are holding on to
> human traditions."
>
> —MARK 7:6–8

Human tradition teaches that a woman is supposed to be virtuous but a man is held to a lesser standard. Over time this mentality developed into tolerance for men refusing to uphold their agreements when it came to marriage. A man was free to have sex with a woman, a concubine, but he did not have to take her as a wife. There was an acceptance for sinning in the manner of making women into concubines because, "It could be worse." Since the men were not participating in outright prostitution and treated the concubine "like" a wife, they became dulled to the fact that they were not upholding God's standards.

The Levites were chosen to uphold the law of God, which gave them a certain status among the people of Israel.

> I have taken the Levites from among the Israelites in place of the first male offspring of every Israelite woman. The Levites are mine.
>
> —NUMBERS 3:12

For a Levite to obtain a concubine, which is part of man's laws, sets an example of condoning and upholding man's law alongside God's law.

> Thus you nullify the word of God by your tradition that you have handed down. And you do many things like that.
>
> —MARK 7:13

In Judges chapter 19, the woman leaves the Levite and returns to her father's house. After four months the Levite goes to get her back, and when the woman's father sees him, the father is glad to meet him. This means the father was happy with the arrangement of his daughter living with a man to whom she was not formally married, continuing in tradition rather than a godly marriage. The woman's father does everything he can to get the Levite to stay in his house for as long as possible, but eventually the Levite leaves with his concubine. As they are traveling home, they stop for the night in Gibeah and stay at an old man's house.

> While they were enjoying themselves, some of the wicked men of the city surrounded the house. Pounding on the door, they shouted to the old man who owned the house, "Bring out the man who came to your house so we can have sex with him."
>
> The owner of the house went outside and said to them, "No, my friends, don't be so vile. Since this man is my guest, don't do this outrageous thing. Look, here is my virgin daughter, and his concubine. I will bring them out to you now, and you can use them and do to them whatever you wish. But as for this man, don't do such an outrageous thing."
>
> —Judges 19:22–24

The old man in this story was willing to defend a stranger whom he had just met as opposed to the daughter who was his own seed. In offering his virgin daughter to be raped by the crowd, the old man was releasing her into a covenant of rape. The old man sent a message that his daughter's virginity was worth less than a stranger, and expendable. The old man was only doing what he thought was right, because to him it seemed better for a man to rape a woman than for a man to rape another man. Had he been upholding the Word of God, he would not have offered that compromise, because God's solution to homosexuality was stoning:

If a man has sexual relations with a man as one does with a woman, both of them have done what is detestable. They are to be put to death; their blood will be on their own heads.

—LEVITICUS 20:13

The old man used his authority to potentially release his daughter to a crowd of rapists but cherry-picked his responsibility to protect her and uphold God's law concerning homosexuals.

God places such a high value on virginity that His holy priests, who are ranked highest among his brothers, are required to marry virgins. The old man did not respect his daughter's virginity as holy. Also, the old man's offer included the Levite's concubine.

The high priest, the one among his brothers who has had the anointing oil poured on his head and who has been ordained to wear the priestly garments, must not let his hair become unkempt or tear his clothes. He must not enter a place where there is a dead body. He must not make himself unclean, even for his father or mother, nor leave the sanctuary of his God or desecrate it, because he has been dedicated by the anointing oil of his God. I am the LORD.

The woman he marries must be a virgin. He must not marry a widow, a divorced woman, or a woman defiled by prostitution, but only a virgin from his own people, so that he will not defile his offspring among his people. I am the LORD, who makes him holy.

—LEVITICUS 21:10–15, EMPHASIS ADDED

The Levite then forcefully obliged the offer.

> But the men would not listen to him. So the man
> took his concubine and sent her outside to them,
> and they raped her and abused her throughout the
> night, and at dawn they let her go.
>
> —JUDGES 19:25

The Levite had already denied this woman his formal hand in marriage and ceremony by making her his concubine. It is not certain that he was the one who took her virginity when she became his concubine, but her virginity was not honored in the union because she was not a wife. Then, he cared so little about her that he was willing to throw her out to a crowd to be raped and abused all night long. It can even be speculated that the man was seeking to pay her back for being unfaithful to him. The Levite could not formally charge her by the law, because she was not his wife, but he could take it upon himself to punish her through the violent men of the city. The justification could be, "If you like other men so much, why don't you have a taste of these men?"

The Levite further showed how little he cared about the woman the next morning.

> At daybreak the woman went back to the house
> where her master [husband] was staying, fell down
> at the door and lay there until daylight.
>
> When her master [husband] got up in the
> morning and opened the door of the house and
> stepped out to continue on his way, there lay his
> concubine, fallen in the doorway of the house, with

her hands on the threshold. He said to her, "Get up; let's go." But there was no answer. Then the man put her on his donkey and set out for home.
—JUDGES 19:26–28

In verse 27 the Scripture says, "When her master [husband] got up." So after callously throwing her out to be gang raped and abused by the men of the city, the Levite went to bed. The woman had collapsed at the door at daybreak and lay there until it grew light. The Levite didn't even attempt to make an early start the next morning after being fully aware of the abuse this woman was going through. The man was not even listening out for her return and let her lie out at the door of the house for hours after her brutal rape.

When the Levite found the woman lying at the door, he did not respond with compassion or remorse—just a cold, "Get up; let's go." He was implying that her lying at the door was an act of laziness. After he realized that she was dead, he loaded her onto the donkey, like a mere sake of grain, and took her home. The Scripture never records any moment where this Levite grieved over this woman or accepted any responsibility for her death. Then, having no respect for her body, he did not bury her, but cut her into twelve pieces and sent her to the regions of Israel.

When he reached home, he took a knife and cut up his concubine, limb by limb, into twelve parts and sent them into all the areas of Israel.
—JUDGES 19:29

The people of Israel came to find out what happened. When the Levite gave his explanation, he altered the story and left out parts to make himself appear better than he was.

> So the Levite, the husband of the murdered woman, said, "I and my concubine came to Gibeah in Benjamin to spend the night. During the night the men of Gibeah came after me and surrounded the house, intending to kill me. They raped my concubine, and she died."
>
> —JUDGES 20:4–5

The Levite claimed that he had been attacked by the men of Gibeah, but that never happened. He said the men raped his concubine to death, which was true, but he left out the part where he cast her out to them after the old man offered her up as a rape object. The Levite was lying by only telling the partial truth. Adding that the men had attacked him made it appear as though the Levite had made an attempt to fight, as opposed to the whole truth—that he hid behind his concubine because he was a coward.

Men of Israel hiding behind their wives is a generational iniquity that started with Abraham.

> As he [Abram] was about to enter Egypt, he said to his wife Sarai, "I know what a beautiful woman you are. When the Egyptians see you, they will say, 'This is his wife.' Then they will kill me but will let you live. Say you are my sister, so that I

will be treated well for your sake and my life will
be spared because of you."

—GENESIS 12:11–13

God had just told Abram in verses 1–3 of that same
chapter that He would bless him and make him a great
nation. However, in lack of trust that he would survive
to be made into a great nation, he hid behind his wife,
Sarai, saying that he would stay alive because of her.
Abram was afraid because in his culture it was a
common practice to attack foreigners and rape their
women. Knowing that this could potentially occur,
Abram's plan was to invent a lie that protected him
rather than to defend his wife from this type of attack.
Subjecting Sarai to potential abuse became a substitute
for believing the promise of God.

> When Abram came to Egypt, the Egyptians saw
> that Sarai was a very beautiful woman. And when
> Pharaoh's officials saw her, they praised her to
> Pharaoh, and she was taken into his palace. He
> treated Abram well for her sake, and Abram
> acquired sheep and cattle, male and female don-
> keys, male and female servants, and camels.
>
> —GENESIS 12:14–16

Abram benefited, but no concern was shown for Sarai;
she was taken to Pharaoh's house whether or not she
wanted to be there. There were no details as to what
happened to Sarai after she was taken to Pharaoh's
house. A pious view would be that she was serving obe-
diently, but the truth is that Abram's lack of trust in God
in that moment led to the defilement of their marriage

covenant. God intervened in this situation, inflicting plagues on Pharaoh, so Sarai was returned to Abram, but Abram's behavior planted the seed of generational iniquity.

Immediately Isaac, Abram's son, did exactly the same thing with his wife:

> So Isaac stayed in Gerar. When the men of that place asked him about his wife, he said, "She is my sister," because he was afraid to say, "She is my wife." He thought, "The men of this place might kill me on account of Rebekah, because she is beautiful."
>
> —GENESIS 26:6–7

Situations like this are often justified by saying, "Times were different back then," or "That's just how it was." However, things were "that way" because the men failed to act any differently. The blessing of Abraham had passed to his son Isaac, but in this situation Isaac did not utilize the authority that came from the blessing to defend his wife. He was held captive by his own fear and allowed their marriage covenant to become compromised with the abuse that he was potentially allowing his wife to endure.

The Levite in Judges willfully subjected his concubine to abuse in a manner similar to the way his forefathers did. The Levite told his version of the events to the people of Israel to mitigate the crime:

> The tribes of Israel sent messengers throughout the tribe of Benjamin, saying, "What about this awful crime that was committed among you? Now

turn those wicked men of Gibeah over to us so
that we may put them to death and purge the evil
from Israel." But the Benjamites would not listen
to their fellow Israelites.

—JUDGES 20:12–13

Putting the guilty men to death for murder was the
correct thing to do. However, the people of Benjamin
refused to allow justice to be administered. This is called
enabling. By gathering an army to fight against the other
tribes of Israel, the people were defending and justifying
the behavior of rapists and murderers.

When God made the covenant with Israel for the land,
they had to fight for it. Fighting to defend the rights of
known rapists and murderers is making a covenant with
them. It is also breaking the covenant with God.

Anyone who kills a person is to be put to death
as a murderer only on the testimony of witnesses.
But no one is to be put to death on the testimony
of only one witness.

—NUMBERS 35:30

There were witnesses, and a murder, but Benjamin
refused to put the guilty to death. Pacifying the guilty
can be done in subtle ways that justify rape as a cultural
norm.

Modern sayings such as "Boys will be boys" set an
expectation that boys are naturally destructive, and
because of their nature as boys they are not in control
or accountable for their actions.

In Judges 19:20, the old man urged the Levite and his
concubine not to stay on the street. The old man's strong

urging came from a sense that it was unsafe to stay on the street. So we see that violence in the streets was already established as normal. The people had become so accustomed to the violence that rather than confronting it, they acquiesced to it. They set a standard that people should not stay out in the street, therefore handing over authority to the offenders to commit violence in the street.

Now, backed by the authority of the people who acted as enablers, blame could be placed on the victim for being on the street. When the victim can be blamed for the violence done to her, it becomes nearly impossible for the guilty to be held responsible. Subtle behavior such as deeming an area unsafe is the first step in shifting the blame to the innocent party. The people of Benjamin defended the rapists and murderers because their culture had been inundated with the belief that these men had done nothing wrong because the women had crossed the criminals' authority to commit violence in the streets.

The people of Benjamin were in covenant with violence. This type of agreement is found in any culture where it is generally accepted that it is not safe for women to go out alone at night. Rather than holding the men who commit violence against women accountable, the culture becomes an enabler by making covenants with violence where the victim is blamed for the violence committed against her. If a woman is raped at a party, society shifts the blame to her for simply being out at night, or for putting herself in a position to be raped. Terms of modesty are applied not in a sense of humility, but to blame the woman.

It is a common saying that it takes two to tango, implying that there have to be two people involved in sin and that the guilt is shared. However, rape is one of the few sins where one party holds 100 percent of the liability.

> But if out in the country a man happens to meet a young woman pledged to be married and rapes her, only the man who has done this shall die. Do nothing to the woman; she has committed no sin deserving death. This case is like that of someone who attacks and murders a neighbor, for the man found the young woman out in the country, and though the betrothed woman screamed, there was no one to rescue her.
>
> —DEUTERONOMY 22:25–27

The scripture compares rape to murder, yet people tend to trivialize the effects of rape and refuse to enforce the penalty for the crime.

Today, sex offenders receive jail time for rape as a substitute for the death penalty. Depending on the level of violence involved in the rape, an offender can serve as little as five months in prison. Weak sentencing of sexual offenders shows a lack of concern when it comes to enforcing the fitting penalty for the crime, or denial that a serious crime has taken place. This is exactly the same way the people of Benjamin refused to acknowledge that a horrendous crime had taken place by not handing over the men who gang raped, brutalized, and murdered a woman.

The concubine in Judges was not a virtuous woman. Therefore, her case against the men of Gibeah who raped and murdered her was weakened by a culture that is inclined to consider her the initiator of the violence. Her lack of virtue was also set up by man-made rules that both condoned and condemned sex outside of marriage. Sex outside of marriage was condoned by the man-made concubine system. But the concubine was condemned because she was expected to uphold the laws that bound her to be like a wife without receiving any benefits from the man. This is the same way the men of Israel treated God's covenant with them. They expected to obtain blessings from God, but without formally dedicating themselves to upholding His law. By shifting back and forth between God's Word and what they thought was right, an alternate covenant was created.

When the people of Israel finally consulted God, He told them to fight against the Benjamites. It took three tries before the army of Israel could defeat the tribe of Benjamin. Then, after the battle had been won, the men of Israel made a rash vow:

> The men of Israel had taken an oath at Mizpah: "Not one of us will give his daughter in marriage to a Benjamite."
> —JUDGES 21:1

This would seem like it was done out of protection, knowing the character of Benjamites, but it became a snare for more violence. Immediately after making this rash vow, the men of Israel began lamenting over losing one of the tribes of Israel.

> The people went to Bethel, where they sat before God until evening, raising their voices and

weeping bitterly. "LORD, God of Israel," they cried,
"why has this happened to Israel? Why should one
tribe be missing from Israel today?"

—JUDGES 21:2–3

In response to the rash vow, the men decided that
they should raid the town of Jabesh Gilead and take
the women there. This town was supposed to be taken
as part of the Promised Land, but taking possession of
the Promised Land at this point was an afterthought,
and reactionary. The warriors of Benjamin were more
willing to use their strength to defend rapists and
murderers than to take the land God had ordered
them to take.

> You are about to cross the Jordan to enter and
> take possession of the land the LORD your God is
> giving you. When you have taken it over and are
> living there, be sure that you obey all the decrees
> and laws I am setting before you today.
>
> —DEUTERONOMY 11:31–32

There was also a protocol for the treatment of women
who were prisoners of war in Deuteronomy chapter 21,
but the halfhearted, lackadaisical methods in which the
men of Israel were upholding God's Word leaves room
to believe that they did not follow this procedure—especially knowing that the Benjamites' purpose for taking
Jabesh Gilead was to get women and not to honor God's
decree to take the Promised Land.

> "How can we provide wives for those who are
> left, since we have taken an oath by the Lord not
> to give them any of our daughters in marriage?"

121

Then they asked, "Which one of the tribes of Israel
failed to assemble before the Lord at Mizpah?"
They discovered that no one from Jabesh Gilead
had come to the camp for the assembly. For when
they counted the people, they found that none of
the people of Jabesh Gilead were there.
So the assembly sent twelve thousand fighting
men with instructions to go to Jabesh Gilead and
put to the sword those living there, including the
women and children. "This is what you are to do,"
they said. "Kill every male and every woman who is
not a virgin." They found among the people living
in Jabesh Gilead four hundred young women who
had never slept with a man, and they took them to
the camp at Shiloh in Canaan.
Then the whole assembly sent an offer of peace
to the Benjamites at the rock of Rimmon. So the
Benjamites returned at that time and were given
the women of Jabesh Gilead who had been spared.
But there were not enough for all of them.

—Judges 21:7–14

God was not consulted in the decision that the four
hundred women from Jabesh Gilead were not enough.
Benjamin started out as one person, Rachel's youngest
son, and therefore it would not be impossible for the
tribe to rebuild with just four hundred women and those
who remained after the war. The men ignored the possibility that the small numbers in the tribes of Benjamin
was actually a divine punishment for the tribe coming
together to defend rape and murder.

But when grace is shown to the wicked, they do not
learn righteousness; even in a land of uprightness

they go on doing evil and do not regard the maj-
esty of the LORD.

—ISAIAH 26:10

Israel chose the path of pity, enabling the wicked,
rather than judging so the Benjamites could have
learned what righteousness was. In another reactionary
response to the rash vow the men of Israel made to not
allow the men of Benjamin marry their daughters, they
ordered the Benjamites to forcefully take wives so the
men could keep their vows.

> "But look, there is the annual festival of the LORD
> in Shiloh, which lies north of Bethel, east of the
> road that goes from Bethel to Shechem, and south
> of Lebonah."
>
> So they instructed the Benjamites, saying, "Go
> and hide in the vineyards and watch. When the
> young women of Shiloh come out to join in the
> dancing, rush from the vineyards and each of you
> seize one of them to be your wife. Then return
> to the land of Benjamin. When their fathers or
> brothers complain to us, we will say to them, 'Do
> us the favor of helping them, because we did not
> get wives for them during the war. You will not be
> guilty of breaking your oath because you did not
> give your daughters to them.'"
>
> So that is what the Benjamites did. While the
> young women were dancing, each man caught
> one and carried her off to be his wife. Then they
> returned to their inheritance and rebuilt the
> towns and settled in them.
>
> —JUDGES 21:19–23

The fathers honored their words more than their daughters. They were quick to disregard any agreements they made with the Lord in terms of following the law, but were not able to break their word when it came to the rape of their daughters. Yeshua addressed this issue in His Sermon on the Mount.

> Again, you have heard that it was said to the people long ago, "Do not break your oath, but fulfill to the Lord the vows you have made." But I tell you, do not swear an oath at all: either by heaven, for it is God's throne; or by the earth, for it is his footstool; or by Jerusalem, for it is the city of the Great King. And do not swear by your head, for you cannot make even one hair white or black. All you need to say is simply "Yes" or "No"; anything beyond this comes from the evil one.
>
> —MATTHEW 5:33–37

God is the one who makes a nation great or small, not the number of women available. The evil root in the men of Israel's decision to allow the Benjamites to forcefully carry away their daughters was condoning the belief that it was acceptable to rape women for the sake of building a nation, rather than depending on God. Vows put men in the place of God; a vow is a guarantee of a certain event or thing, and in his own power, man cannot guarantee anything. Therefore, men have sought methods that are very ungodly in an attempt to guarantee their word, even allowing rape.

This type of thinking occurs because the effects of rape tended to be trivialized. Rape is a man-made, deliberate, and malicious act that causes the victim to experience anxiety, nightmares, irritability, guilt, self-blame, cynicism, difficulty concentrating, depression, grief, changes in personality, and many other issues. Preexisting notions of women being emotional in their nature makes it easy for the emotional symptoms of wrongdoing to be discredited.

A woman who has been raped may suffer from irritability, a symptom of unresolved anger from the attack. Her irritability may manifest in the form of intense criticizing, impatience, and heated arguing. Since these behaviors are expected from women, who are deemed emotional in their nature, the root cause of the abuse they have suffered at the hands of men is not addressed. The men of Benjamin could carry on in marriages with women they kidnapped and raped because the supposed emotional disposition of women cancels out their reactions as symptoms of trauma.

The effects of rape can be trivialized so easily because marriage, sex, and women are often taken so lightly. The trivialization of marriage was manifested the strongest in the patriarch Jacob in the generational iniquity from his fathers, Abraham and Isaac. When Jacob traveled to Haran, he met Rachel and agreed to work for her father, Laban, seven years for her dowry. What is often misunderstood is that the dowry is not for the sale of a daughter, but is intended as a security. The money that is paid for a bride is for her father to keep in the event that the groom rejects her, so if she returns to her father's home, the dowry is there for her provision. However, Laban used the dowry as a bartering tool for his own personal profit.

So Laban brought together all the people of the place and gave a feast. But when evening came, he took his daughter Leah and brought her to Jacob, and Jacob made love to her. And Laban gave his servant Zilpah to his daughter as her attendant.

When morning came, there was Leah! So Jacob said to Laban, "What is this you have done to me? I served you for Rachel, didn't I? Why have you deceived me?"

Laban replied, "It is not our custom here to give the younger daughter in marriage before the older one. Finish this daughter's bridal week; then we will give you the younger one also, in return for another seven years of work."

—GENESIS 29:22–27

Laban used the dowry from the marriage of his daughters as a bartering tool for monetary gain. Afterwards, Laban spent all the money that was intended for his daughters' protection. When Jacob consulted with his wives about leaving, they agreed to leave with him, following the promise of God. But if they had wanted to stay, it would have been impossible, because Laban had spent the dowry that was intended for them.

Then Rachel and Leah replied, "Do we still have any share in the inheritance of our father's estate? Does he not regard us as foreigners? Not only has he sold us, but he has used up what was paid for us."

—GENESIS 31:14–15

By consuming the dowry that was meant for his daughters, Laban cut them out of any inheritance from their father's household. In this way it would appear that only a son could have an inheritance. When the father does not protect the dowry, marriage becomes a transaction as though a wife is a possession to be bought, which significantly decreases the respect a woman receives in the household. The Levite in Judges was supportive of the men treating his concubine like a rape object because with this type of mind-set he already considered the woman a sex object.

Without proper use of the dowry, sex becomes a weapon or asset based on a monetary system. As a result, women and marriage are trivialized because they are merely bought and sold. The event of rape becomes like an attack on a man's assets instead of a personal attack against another human being.

There was a clear agreement between Jacob and Laban, but Laban overtly disregarded the agreement when he brought Leah into the marriage. Laban used the attractiveness of Rachel as collateral and bait to get Jacob to work for a dowry, which Laban would spend on himself. In order for the plan to take place, Leah had to be aware that it was Rachel who Jacob wanted. Yet Laban, Leah's father, released her into the covenant knowing that she was not wanted. Leah's thoughts and feelings were completely trivialized when her father enacted the plan. With Rachel being the more attractive sister, Laban further demoralized Leah by sending the message that she had to settle for being part of a polygamous relationship because she was not good enough for a monogamous marriage.

Leah would spend a significant portion of the marriage seeking love from a man who was closed off to her because she was treated as a mere money-making tool for her father. Leah gave Jacob seven children, which of course had to be the result of intercourse, but because her position in the relationship was that of a possession bought with money, Jacob could have intercourse with her and remain emotionally distant without question. The seventh child of Leah was a daughter named Dinah, meaning "controversy over rights." The name would fit perfectly with the circumstances of her life after she was raped.

> Now Dinah, the daughter Leah had borne to Jacob, went out to visit the women of the land. When Shechem son of Hamor the Hivite, the ruler of that area, saw her, he took her and raped her.
> —Genesis 34:1–2

After Shechem raped Dinah, he decided that he wanted to marry her, and offered to pay a huge bride price. Then, after agreeing to become circumcised, Jacob accepted the union. Repeating the circumstances of Leah, Dinah was not given any say in the relationship, and the dowry was treated as a sales transaction. Because the emotions and will of her mother, Leah, were so easily disregarded, Dinah was in prime condition to be treated the same way, even in the event of rape.

To further justify the horrendous affront to Dinah's rights, there had to be a cultural guilt shift. She had been traveling alone; therefore, the culture had to adjust to make it inappropriate for her to be alone, to put her at fault. Shechem saw her and then raped her; therefore, a woman's looks had to be brought into a systematic control of modesty. It is not the biblical modesty of humble behavior, but man-made guilt and shame associated with man's potential to rape and abuse if he takes notice of a woman's beauty.

A low-grade form of shame-based, man-made modesty is street harassment. Street harassment involves unsolicited compliments, cat-calling, derogatory comments, rude stares, and other inappropriate verbal and mental abuse of women who are passing by on the street. Street harassment is used as a tool to exert sexual aggression based on a woman's appearance. The goal is to show utter contempt for the fact that the woman has simply left the house, and it is covered by the fast pace in which the crime occurs. A man blurting out, "Hey baby," in a husky voice takes only a few seconds and its malicious intent is virtually unprovable.

A woman cannot do anything about a lustful look. A street harasser knows about this. So a man stares at a woman in a manner that is openly sexual with the intent to make her into a second-class citizen. Society leaves one of two options on the extreme scale. The first is to do nothing, meaning the woman has a lesser right to be in public comfortably. The next option is seen in Islamic countries where if a man looks at a woman for more than five seconds he has to marry her.[1] This option offers some prevention for the street harasser's leer, but it does not account for the repercussions against a woman who is simply in the market and is looked at by a man, and is forced into marriage.

God has an opinion of the openly lustful gaze, which Yeshua addressed.

> But I tell you that anyone who looks at a woman
> lustfully has already committed adultery with
> her in his heart. If your right eye causes you to
> stumble, gouge it out and throw it away. It is
> better for you to lose one part of your body than
> for your whole body to be thrown into hell. And
> if your right hand causes you to stumble, cut it off
> and throw it away. It is better for you to lose one
> part of your body than for your whole body to go
> into hell.
>
> —MATTHEW 5:28–30

Yeshua identified that a lustful glance is a tremendous sin. Rather than placing the blame on the woman for supposedly "arousing" the man's lust, doing nothing, or forcing a marriage upon her, He said that the man would be better off gouging out his eye if he could not control his glance. Yeshua said it was better to lose the eye than for the whole body go to hell, meaning leering at a woman is an offense that makes one hellbound. Then He spoke about the same concept for the right hand, which in context would apply to self-gratification on the sight of a woman also being a "hellbound" offense. For society to force the blame on the woman or ignore how problematic street harassment is, is another compromise in following God in exchange for a rape covenant.

The unwritten rule of street harassment is that it almost never occurs when a woman is escorted by a man. The fact that it is not done when there is a male witness present shows that street harassment is intentional, in effect. In the most extreme cases of this, women in Islamic countries must cover their bodies entirely and are forbidden to leave their homes without a man present. The Quran says that women should stay in their homes:

> And abide quietly in your homes, and do not flaunt your charms as they used to flaunt them in the old days of pagan ignorance; and be consistent in prayer, and render the purifying dues, and pay heed to Allah and his messenger: for Allah wants only to remove you from all that might be loathsome, O you members of the (prophets) household, and to purify you to upmost purity.
>
> —SURAH AL-AHZAB 33:33

Paired with the laws that require a male escort for a woman to leave the house, it is implied that leaving the house alone qualifies her as a whore and fair game for attack.

This mentality continues through the body of believers through shame-based modesty and strict religious observances that are compatible with Islam.

When low-grade harassment becomes a cultural norm, women come to expect it and are far less likely to consider it out of place. The physiological effects of rape will cause the victim to blame herself for the violence done to her, so she may try to make herself look unattractive to avoid street harassment, placate society by submitting to the unwritten rule to always be escorted by a man, or avoid areas where men are known to harass. Women learn to ignore the behavior rather than address it. If a woman attempts to combat it, she is viewed as a raging disgruntled person picking a fight over a man simply "complimenting" her.

When a torturer boils someone alive, he does not raise the temperature directly to boiling. He begins with a comfortable water temperature, then raises it to a high point, and then lowers it back down to the initial temperature.[2] This causes the one being tortured to become used to the higher temperatures. In this manner, the one being tortured builds a tolerance, which causes the torture to endure longer.

Street harassment opens the door for men to gradually increase the level of sexual violence. Women build tolerance for sexual aggression when they expect street harassment, so it is not as noticeable when men further encroach on their rights. A man may inappropriately brush against a woman in a crowded room and there is no one to enforce the fact that his brief touch was intentional and a crime against her. Young boys, starting around the age of twelve, treat pinching a girl's buttocks and running away as a game. Since this behavior begins just as a girl begins to develop physically, it is training for her to be helpless against the continuation of this and greater types of sexual offense.

Rape slowly becomes an expectation that a woman has to deal with. With an expectation of violence, little is to be done about the problem. For example, Dinah was a victim to the expectation that a man could look at her, abuse her, and then accept no accountability for what he did because of his sexual desire. When shame-based modesty is used as a remedy for the problem among Bible believers, it makes the customs and practices of the Quran and Islam indistinguishable from the Word of God.

Behaviors such as street harassment can be brushed off as simple immaturity or unintentional offense—applying the "Boys will be boys" rule—or a man's simple inability to express his desire in a constructive manner. However, street harassment is a common occurrence, and it is well known that women do not like it. Since it is well known that most women find it uncomfortable, it is clear that street harassment is a forceful and malicious act that is only covered by subtlety.

After he raped Dinah, Shechem used the same tactic of pretending to be unaware of the harmful effects of his actions and claiming that it was only out of misplaced affection that he raped her.

> His heart was drawn to Dinah daughter of Jacob;
> he loved the young woman and spoke tenderly to
> her. And Shechem said to his father Hamor, "Get
> me this girl as my wife."
> —GENESIS 34:3–4

The proposal of marriage is only a façade of purity. In biblical law, sex is only supposed to take place within marriage. Now that a sexual act had taken place against Dinah's will, her lack of purity was solely the fault of Shechem. To introduce another shift in blame, maintaining the appearance of Dinah's purity took precedence over addressing the rape. The marriage proposal also gave the appearance that the exchange between Dinah and Shechem was sex that was out of place rather than a violent act of sexual aggression imposed upon her.

> Then Shechem said to Dinah's father and brothers,
> "Let me find favor in your eyes, and I will give you

> whatever you ask. Make the price for the bride and
> the gift I am to bring as great as you like, and I'll
> pay whatever you ask me. Only give me the young
> woman as my wife."
>
> —GENESIS 34:11–12

Shechem's offering to pay a large bride price makes
it appear as though he is making a huge sacrifice to be
with Dinah because he cares so much, yet again trivial-
izing the rape he committed against her as misplaced
affection. Also, in paying a large bride price, the dowry
is treated as a sales transaction as recompense for dam-
aging the father's valuable asset of a beautiful virgin
daughter, rather than being set aside as an inheritance
for her if she is rejected by her husband. Now, there is
no distinction between a whore and a wife. The most
common defense of the rapist is the claim that the
woman is a whore and really wanted it. By making Dinah
into a whore of a wife bought with money, Shechem
cleared himself of all wrongdoing.

A marriage obligates the man to support the woman
with food, clothing, and shelter. If a man marries a
woman after raping her, it gives the appearance that he
is doing her a favor. He is saving the child she could
potentially bear as a result of the rape from being a bastard, as well as giving support to the woman although
she is defiled.

It was very difficult for a woman to get a husband if
she was not a virgin, so Shechem may have made himself believe he was saving Dinah from becoming a concubine or an old maid. If her father, Jacob, had refused
the marriage, the bride price would be given to Dinah

for lifetime support to compensate for the damage that was done to her. However, the bride price had been prostituted not to include the daughter. Dinah was denied restitution for the violence done to her, and left to either live in shame or marry the man who raped her.

Eventually, Dinah's brothers, Levi and Simeon, took vengeance by killing all the males of Shechem, and snatched Dinah out of Shechem's house. The fact that she was living in Shechem's house brings up doubt as to how brutal the attack on her really was. Causing doubt was the exact intention of Shechem's actions, and shame the main motivator in controlling Dinah. Had Dinah stayed with Shechem, he would have likely had free rein to establish a pattern of abuse. If her initial rape was never addressed, spousal rape would be impossible to contend against. The outer form of purity of "sex" within the marriage would cover the violent acts that would take place behind closed doors.

When maintaining an outward form of purity, an open discussion of sex does not occur. Silence becomes a safeguard for an abusive man. In modern culture, women tend not to report rape out of a sense of shame. This shame factor is increased if the woman was in a relationship with the man prior to the attack, or in a compromising position during the attack, such as being in a man's room, drunk, not a virgin, etc. Outward purity makes light of how high the statistics are concerning sexual violence against women.

Proving spousal rape in any case is difficult because marriage in itself represents consent. In order to open the door to unquestioned spousal rape, neglect, and violence, a man circumvents the authority of the daughter, going directly to the father with a large dowry, which is used as a purchase as opposed to her inheritance.

> A good person leaves an inheritance for their children's children.
>
> —PROVERBS 13:22

A father may be predisposed to agree to sell his daughter because of his views toward sex and women through his relationship with his wives or extramarital concubines. Supporting a daughter, which a father is obligated to do under biblical law, is a liability to his finances. Therefore, releasing her into a covenant by sale frees him of his responsibility to her and offers him capital gain. Abuse and rape in marriage might be accepted because he himself treats women the same way—passively, in emotional abuse and neglect, like in Leah's case; or openly, through physical and sexual abuse, as was the case with Dinah.

The way a father treats his wife is an indication of how he will treat his daughter. Leah was not intentionally harmed by Jacob, but she was loved less. Dinah was not intentionally neglected by Jacob, but was considered lesser in the household in comparison to her brothers. A father's actions may be defended by claiming that all men love their daughters and the old man in Judges, the concubine's father, and Jacob are merely extreme cases. However, observing the common mistreatment of women in Muslim countries and unequal rights of women in the name of Christian theology over the centuries shows the opposite. Each of these women who were denied rights was someone's daughter.

Saul, the first king of Israel, from the tribe of Benjamin, continued the rape covenant by misusing the dowry and arranging an illegal marriage for his daughter. After Saul failed to be obedient to God, David was anointed to be king. Saul was extremely jealous and wanted to kill David. After Saul found out that his daughter Michal loved David, he exploited the feelings she had for him. Instead of a dowry, Saul requested that David bring him the foreskins of one hundred Philistines, intending for David to be killed in battle. Saul had no regard for his daughter's feelings, and also used the dowry, which was meant for her protection and inheritance, as a tool against a perceived enemy.

David was successful in battle and was able to marry Michal. However, David had to flee from Saul to keep from being murdered. Because Michal's dowry had been paid in foreskins, after David fled she had no independent support. She would have to return to her father, Saul, who then gave her to another man.

> But Saul had given his daughter Michal, David's wife, to Paltiel son of Laish, who was from Gallim.
> —1 SAMUEL 25:44

This was an illegal union because David was still alive. She was not a widow, nor had David divorced her. By using marriage as a tool for his separate agenda, Saul made his daughter into an adulteress. Saul used his authority as a father to force his daughter to break the law of God. The fact that Saul was in authority made it difficult for his daughter to distinguish between God's law and her father's law, because children are supposed to honor their parents.

God also gave specific commands to fathers showing that they could not use their authority for their own purpose.

> Do not degrade your daughter by making her a prostitute, or the land will turn to prostitution and be filled with wickedness.
> —LEVITICUS 19:29

A father who squanders a dowry sells his daughter, which makes her a prostitute. Forcing her to marry another man when becoming angry at a son-in-law makes her a prostitute. Any type of forced marriage is prostitution. It is further addressed in the New Testament how fathers are not to misuse their authority.

> And you, fathers, do not provoke your children to wrath [and make them resentful], but bring them up in the training and admonition of the Lord.
> —EPHESIANS 6:4, NKJV

The resentment that Michal felt became apparent when she was reunited with David.

> As the ark of the covenant of the LORD was entering the City of David, Michal daughter of Saul watched from a window. And when she saw King David dancing and celebrating, she despised him in her heart.
> —1 CHRONICLES 15:29

Michal had been passed around from husband to husband because of her father. The Scripture also says in Deuteronomy 24 that it is unlawful for a woman to return to her first husband after she has been with another husband. After being denied the basic rights to not be treated like a sex possession and to be able to follow the law, Michal was unable to function in a relationship with someone whom she had once loved, possibly because she could not separate the resentment she had toward her father from her feelings toward other men.

The matriarch Rebekah was asked if she would go with the man who was seeking a groom for her. This practice of mutual agreement was lost among the descendants of Israel in replacement for condoned rape, or degradation of daughters in marriage. Instances like Saul debasing his daughter teach other fathers that they are above the law. However, there is such a strong move to teach otherwise, because men have been habitually trying to show that their authority makes them above the law, and not that their authority is given only to uphold the law.

> Do not think that I have come to abolish the Law or the Prophets; I have not come to abolish them but to fulfill them. For truly I tell you, until heaven and earth disappear, not the smallest letter, not the least stroke of a pen, will by any means disappear from the Law until everything is accomplished. Therefore anyone who sets aside one of the least of these commands and teaches others accordingly will be called least in the kingdom of heaven, but whoever practices and

teaches these commands will be called great in the kingdom of heaven.

—MATTHEW 5:17–19

A whore uses sex for her own personal gain. The whore is disdained not because of God's law concerning prostitution, but because she is viewed as denying the father's perceived right to profit from her marriage.

Today there is an epidemic of fornication. This may be triggered by the idea that to women, marriage has come to represent rape and a high form of domestic slavery. Also, fornication among women may indicate that fathers are not giving their daughters enough attention. Worldly women often do not respond to teachings on biblical purity because the teachings themselves have been prostituted to the point that women are simply whores for their fathers' personal gain. This concept can be confirmed in the writings of the prophet Hosea.

> I will not punish your daughters when they turn to prostitution, nor your daughters-in-law when they commit adultery, because the men themselves consort with harlots and sacrifice with shrine prostitutes—a people without understanding will come to ruin!
>
> —HOSEA 4:14

Failing to keep God's Word is often referred to as adultery. When men place themselves above God's Word by forcing their daughters to do something unlawful, the men are in a state of adultery.

Contrary to God's teachings, many cultures believe the woman is the main offender in whoring. Without an understanding of the man's significant role in adultery and prostitution, people come to ruin. Spreading the truth of the gospel is hindered because the hypocrisy is easily refuted by any unbeliever.

> Anyone who does not provide for their relatives, and especially for their own household, has denied the faith and is worse than an unbeliever.
>
> —1 TIMOTHY 5:8

Someone who chooses not to follow God and then behaves wickedly does not reflect poorly on the truth. However, someone who pretends to be righteous opens the door to a rape covenant, and distorts the truth. Shechem intended to do this by forcefully marrying into the chosen people of God. Shechem was a Hivite, the very people God would tell the nation of Israel to destroy after the Exodus from Egypt. The promise of the destruction of the Hivites was given to Abraham.

> When the LORD your God brings you into the land you are entering to possess and drives out before you many nations—the Hittites, Girgashites, Amorites, Canaanites, Perizzites, Hivites and Jebusites, seven nations larger and stronger than you—and when the LORD your God has delivered them over to you and you have defeated them, then you must destroy them totally. Make no treaty with them, and show them no mercy. Do not intermarry with them. Do not give your

daughters to their sons or take their daughters for
your sons

—DEUTERONOMY 7:1–3

Throughout the Scripture, God commanded the children of Israel not to make covenants or intermarry with the Hivites and other nations. By raping Dinah, the daughter of Jacob, Shechem was forcefully trying to make himself a part of the covenant of Abraham, Isaac, and Jacob.

> But Hamor said to them, "My son Shechem has his heart set on your daughter. Please give her to him as his wife. Intermarry with us; give us your daughters and take our daughters for yourselves. You can settle among us; the land is open to you. Live in it, trade in it, and acquire property in it."
>
> —GENESIS 34:8–10

This is directly contrary to what God said. Jacob's agreeing to the marriage between Dinah and Shechem was not only blatant disregard to the honor and rights of his daughter, but also a compromise of what God had said.

After Levi and Simeon avenged their sister, Jacob was angry with them.

> Then Jacob said to Simeon and Levi, "You have brought trouble on me by making me obnoxious to the Canaanites and Perizzites, the people living in this land. We are few in number, and if they join forces against me and attack me, I and my household will be destroyed."
>
> —GENESIS 34:30

Jacob was willing to compromise his daughter's rights because he was afraid of the people. However, God had told Jacob that He would guard him wherever he went, and that he would be given the Promised Land.

> There above it stood the LORD, and he said: "I am the LORD, the God of your father Abraham and the God of Isaac. I will give you and your descendants the land on which you are lying. Your descendants will be like the dust of the earth, and you will spread out to the west and to the east, to the north and to the south. All peoples on earth will be blessed through you and your offspring. I am with you and will watch over you wherever you go, and I will bring you back to this land. I will not leave you until I have done what I have promised you."
>
> —GENESIS 28:13–15

Had Jacob trusted that God would guard him, he would not have been angry with Levi and Simeon, who had taken the first initiative to claim the Promised Land by attacking Shechem. Levi and Simeon were the first Hebrews to war for the Promised Land. Once again the women were compromised because of the man's lack of trust. Jacob cursed Levi and Simeon for killing the Hivite men of Shechem. That curse would set a precedent of Israel shrinking back from taking the Promised Land. This was evident in the way annexing the town of Jabesh Gilead to the Promised Land was an afterthought, and many other events where Israel compromised with the people they were meant to destroy.

The same compromise was present in Judges with the old man feeling as though it was better for his daughter to be raped than for men to be sodomized. The place where Dinah was raped was named after the man who raped her, Shechem. She was released into a covenant of rape by her father. Shechem was the very same place where the men permitted the men of Benjamin to rape women and carry them off as captives to make them wives:

> "But look, there is the annual festival of the LORD in Shiloh, which lies north of Bethel, east of the road that goes from Bethel to Shechem, and south of Lebonah."
> So they instructed the Benjamites, saying, "Go and hide in the vineyards and watch. When the young women of Shiloh come out to join in the dancing, rush from the vineyards and each of you seize one of them to be your wife. Then return to the land of Benjamin."
> —JUDGES 21:19–21

The rapes that occurred in Shechem renewed Dinah's controversy over rights generations later when the Benjamites felt free to treat other daughters of Jacob (Israel) in the same reckless manner, encroaching on their right to say no to a man.

Dinah never received an inheritance from her father. Part of this was based on her inability to defend herself from someone forcefully taking the inheritance from her. Women are taught to stay in groups for safety. This constant need to be around people may condition women to follow the crowd and be people pleasers. This could cause women to lack leadership skills, which could be used as further justification to deny them respect in marriage, and an inheritance.

The fear of men is often the instigator of indecisive behavior in women. Because of the pending fear of rape and the necessity to stay in groups to avoid it, people pleasing can become a defense mechanism. If the people around a woman are not pleased, she could be abandoned and therefore left vulnerable to attack.

A woman who is subject to her husband in a covenant of rape often makes pleasing him her main purpose in the marriage in order to defend herself against abandonment and possible physical rape. Even if her husband is never violent to her, the fear of other men can be used as a tool to manipulate and control, because if she is not pleasing him, her husband could divorce her and subject her to potential violence.

An unstable father who sold his daughter into marriage by misappropriating the dowry would provide no support against a poor or abusive husband. So even if the husband is not committed to extreme behavior such as rape, the rape covenant may still be present. Small instances of unloving behavior are not addressed, because the wife is bonded to her husband out of fear of worse possibilities.

The husband in a rape covenant is protected from any accountability if intercourse within a marriage is boring, effortless, or unsatisfying in general. This is a lead-in to female genital mutilation, which is a popular practice in Muslim countries. The woman is not expected to enjoy intercourse, and she then becomes obligated to not enjoy intercourse in a rape-dominated culture where men are not accountable for anything they do within a marriage. The man is also not held accountable for emotional, economic, or other forms of abuse. A woman's submissiveness to her husband becomes an act of codependence.

When a man shifts the responsibility for emotional and economic neglect, he does not develop a personal relationship with his wife. Without a close connection to her, a marriage simply becomes an agreement based on sexual and labor services. Therefore, any woman could fill the role of cooking, cleaning, and personal prostitution. This is why polygamist marriages and concubines appeal to men who seek to justify themselves.

When God created humanity, He created them male and female, not male and females. In God's perfect plan, there was no polygamy. After sin entered the world and humanity was corrupted, the men continued the corruption by further separating themselves from God's perfect plan.

When Paul wrote letters concerning the selection of leaders among the believing community, he emphasized the importance of a man being married to one woman:

> If a man is blameless, the husband of one wife, having faithful children not accused of dissipation or insubordination.
>
> —TITUS 1:6, NKJV

Having multiple wives carries the undertones of emotional and economic abuse that denies both parties the type of intimacy necessary for having an intimate relationship with God.

Also, when a husband denies his wife a personal relationship, the sexual act becomes solely an act of physical release. All women then become vessels for sexual gratification. When a woman is attractive but does not offer instant gratification, the man might become angry. He may engage in street harassment to vent his anger, because he knows he cannot act on his sexual impulses, and punishes the strange woman for inadvertently making him feel powerless. Men also punish women by denying them the ability to own possessions such as land or other assets, because they are angry that a woman's possession of land and assets frees her from giving him sexual favors on demand because of her dependence upon him. Rape is used as a tool against a woman, treating her with utter contempt for denying a man instant gratification.

Dinah, a female, was in possession of a heritage from God. Shechem was trying to take the birthright of Israel by forcefully intermarrying. If Dinah had a child as a result of Shechem's rape, it would technically be a bastard and a Hivite, disqualified from standing in the presence of God. Since men are viewed as the warring population, the law of brute force is applied in how the population is ranked, honored, and respected. Dinah was viewed to be beneath her brothers because she was not physically strong like them. However, the use of brute force is in opposition to how God functions. The battles to obtain the promises of God are not won by size or might, but by the level of trust in God.

David's victory over Goliath was won by trust. Gideon defeated the combined forces of the Midianites and Amalekites, who numbered beyond counting, with only three hundred men because the Lord was with him. In Judges chapter 4, the commander of the Canaanite army, Sisera, was defeated by a woman with a tent peg because the people cried out to God. God even chose Israel as His heritage based on their weakness:

> The LORD did not set his affection on you and choose you because you were more numerous than other peoples, for you were the fewest of all peoples.
>
> —DEUTERONOMY 7:7

This same principle of trust rather than might applies to women in God's covenant. Utilizing brute force, monetary advantages, and subjugating people is how people shift from a covenant of God to a covenant of rape, which is strongly present in Islam.

> Men are in charge of women by right of what Allah has given greater strength one over the other and what they spend for maintenance from their wealth. So righteous women devoutly obedient guarding in the husband's absence what Allah would have them guard. But those wives for whom you fear arrogance—first advise them; then if they persist forsake them in bed; and finally strike them. But if they obey you once more seek no means against them. Indeed Allah is ever exacted and grand.
>
> —QURAN SURAH AN-NISA 4:34

The Quran places men in a position of dominance based on their physical strength. This is the same way Dinah was denied an inheritance based on her inability to physically fend off an attacker, and the way the women in the Book of Judges were mistreated because the men could carry them away against their will. The Quran states that this divine right is given to men by Allah because the man supports the woman financially. The fact that a man provides monetary gain for his household can be used as a tool to treat his wives as prostitutes. There is no accountability on the side of the male, because any quarrel from his wife could result in abandonment or beating. Then, he utilizes her fear of other men as a tool of control in the marriage. Mistreating women in this manner is a departure from the covenant of God.

Using rape and abuse to subjugate women in their marriages is a process. The three main factors in creating a covenant with rape are compromise, victim blaming, and brute force. First, marriage is compromised through extramarital sexual engagements with concubines. The concubine cultural system shifts the attitude toward sex and changes marriage to prostitution. Next, the culture finds various ways to blame the victim while denying the man's accountability, using shame-based modesty and the "boys will be boys" mentality. Then, brute force is applied to women because of their physical weakness, which serves as the basis for denying them an inheritance.

These types of compromises are made in modern culture without people recognizing the ramifications of these actions and what they will later lead to. Street harassment is accepted because "it could be worse." People compromise with viewing pornography because the men are taking out their sexual aggression on the computer screen rather than on actual women. A man could catch his son with a pornographic magazine and instead of punishing him he could say, "At least he's not a homosexual," or "It could be something worse in this day and age." Believing parents compromise with their children by allowing their boyfriends or girlfriends to move in with them, saying, "It's better they do it here than somewhere else." Those living arrangements essentially establish the girlfriend as a concubine the same way the father in Judges was happy to meet the Levite his daughter had shacked up with and wanted them to stay at his house.

Today, fewer and fewer people are getting married. Jacob worked for seven years to pay the dowry for Rachel. If a man does not want to work that long or hard, he can get a concubine for free, because it is not a legal marriage. In order to do this, the man has to make a compromise with the law of God to justify himself. By compromising in terms of marriage, men become conditioned to compromise other aspects of following God, which leads to idolatry.

Hagar was the concubine of Abraham. She bore a son by Abraham named Ishmael. When Sarah, Abraham's legitimate wife, saw Ishmael mocking her son, Isaac, Sarah told Abraham to cast her out. When Abraham went to God about the issue, God said that Sarah was right.

> And [Sarah] said to Abraham, "Get rid of that slave woman and her son, for that woman's son will never share in the inheritance with my son Isaac."

> The matter distressed Abraham greatly because
> it concerned his son. But God said to him, "Do
> not be so distressed about the boy and your
> slave woman. Listen to whatever Sarah tells you,
> because it is through Isaac that your offspring will
> be reckoned."
>
> —GENESIS 21:10–12

God telling Abraham to listen to Sarah about getting rid of his concubine shows that God does not condone men taking concubines.

The result of Abraham's relationship with a concubine was Ishmael, the father of the Arab nations and Islam. Ishmael was not meant to inherit the promise of God with Isaac. The son of the concubine represents men doing what they feel is right, like in Judges, and the son of the legitimate wife represents God's Word. As men compromise on God's Word, the results are submitting to a false religion, Islam, and serving a false God, Allah. When looking into the Quran's positions on rape and women it is found to be exactly the mentality of the men in Judges who had departed from wholeheartedly following the law and God.

> Your wives are a place of sowing seed for you, so
> come to your place of cultivation however you
> wish and put forth for yourselves. And fear Allah
> and know that you will meet him. And give seed
> tidings to the believers.
>
> —QURAN SURAH AL-BAQARAH 2:223

The Quran says that men can approach their wives in any way they wish, condoning spousal rape. This state of mind is exactly how the Benjamites treated the women they took captive as wives. Acceptance of spousal rape is done in the name of Allah.

> Certainly will the believers have succeeded. They who are during their prayer humbly submissive. And they who turn away from ill speech. And they who are observant of zakah. And they who guard their private parts.
> —QURAN SURAH AL-MU'MINUM 23:1-6

In Islam, the woman is responsible for guarding her private parts. She shares in the blame for rape. If a woman is raped in an Islamic country, she could be charged with *zina* (fornication) and put to death. This mind-set was present in the way Dinah was raped and an agreement to marry her rapist was made for the purpose of maintaining an outer form of purity for her failure to guard her private parts.

In a rape covenant, there is no distinction between a wife and a prostitute. In the Book of Genesis we read about an event where Judah had sex with his daughter-in-law, whom at the time he believed to be a prostitute.

> When Judah saw her, he thought she was a prostitute, for she had covered her face.
> —GENESIS 38:15

The very act of a woman covering her face for the sake of shame-based modesty made it clear that she is considered to be a prostitute, meant only for sexual gratification in exchange for economic support and protection from men.

O Prophet, tell your wives and your daughters and
the women of the believers to bring over themselves of their outer garments. This is more suitable that they will be known and not molested.
And ever is Allah forgiving and merciful.

—QURAN SURAH AL-AHZAB 33:59

Shame-based modesty is used as a solution to men
lusting after women. Street harassment and other
sexually aggressive behaviors are ignored because
in this way of thinking women are to blame for the
way men react to them. Islam teaches that men have
uncontrollable thoughts and sexual urges, whereas the
Bible states that men have the power to control their
thoughts.

We demolish arguments and every pretension that
sets itself up against the knowledge of God, and
we take captive every thought to make it obedient
to Messiah.

—2 CORINTHIANS 10:5, NCPE

Rather than encouraging people to take every thought
captive, in a rape covenant women are responsible for
everything, including the inclinations of another, in a
relationship in which they have no power. This is just
like the Levite hiding behind his concubine. She did not
have the strength to fend off the Sodomites who were
intending to rape the man, but the Levite exercised
power over her and threw her out to them. By being
raped she protected her husband, but it was a decision
that was forced upon her. In a rape culture, women are
not given authority to make choices in marriage, levels

of modesty, and how they are treated, but they are expected to constantly keep men's sexual desires at bay and always be pleasing to men.

Rape is always an undertone in many cultures, and only a small breakdown of the social order is needed for this rape culture to be awakened. This was evident during 2005's Hurricane Katrina with the large influx of rapes after the disaster. The common street harasser knew that the authorities were not readily available and then had the opportunity to act out the anger toward women freely in rape.

Another example would be the 2000 Puerto Rican Day Parade attacks, where women were accosted by mobs of men who doused them with water, groped them, made sexually explicit comments toward them, robbed them, and tore their clothes off in public. Over fifty women reported the attacks to nearby officers, who did nothing, assuming the attacks were common street harassment.[3]

The acceptance of the crowd of men who participated in the attacks created an atmosphere to move the gauge of common harassment of women up to fondling and forced exposure in broad daylight.

The Congo is nicknamed "the rape capital of the world" because it experienced such a breakdown in society during wartime that a clinic reported an average of three hundred rape victims a month—and those are only the ones reported.[4]

Wartime rape in all parts of the world is so common that it is barely considered a crime and scantly addressed. These citizens were not serial killers, but average men acting on their misogyny, sexual aggression, and contempt for women, which before the breakdown of society was only expressed subtly.

By condoning concubines, defilement of marriage covenants, denying daughters an inheritance, accepting low-grade sexual harassment, and inadequate punishment of rape, people come into covenant with rape, which is service to Allah. Ideologies such as Chrislam become strongholds, blurring the line between what is cherry-picked out of Scriptures and the truth. Those within the body of believers use the excuse that violence against women is present in the Bible as justification for ignoring these behaviors in modern culture without taking note of how the perpetrators in the Bible were acting against God.

Rape is overlooked and condoned so often because men are not only attacking women personally, but are actually coming against God and His bride. We are all the bride of Yeshua. Yeshua is the High Priest and is required to marry a virgin.

> Therefore, since we have a great high priest who has gone through the heavens, Yeshua the Son of God, let us hold firmly to the faith we profess.
> —HEBREWS 4:14, NCPE

The bride of Yeshua is intentionally being defiled, and the men who are meant to protect the bride are willfully participating in defiling her.

> Husbands, love your wives, just as the Messiah loved the Messianic Community, indeed, gave himself up on its behalf, in order to set it apart for God, making it clean through immersion in

the *mikveh*, so to speak, in order to present the
Messianic Community to himself as a bride to
be proud of, without a spot, wrinkle or any such
thing, but holy and without defect.

—Ephesians 5:25–27, cjb

Presenting a bride without defect means that a man
would not have an emotionally, physically, or sexually battered wife. Rather than having a wife who is
immersed in purity with a husband who would defend
her from attack, she is immersed in a rape culture
where the husband willfully allows violence or the
threat of violence to control her.

Satan intentionally tries to defile Yeshua's bride
through rape to try to keep her from her Groom. The
men who are used in the defilement of the bride are
ready agents of Satan and have forsaken God.

When the dragon saw that he had been hurled to
the earth, he pursued the woman who had given
birth to the male child...

Then the dragon was enraged at the woman
and went off to make war against the rest of her
offspring.

—Revelation 12:13, 17, ncpe

Although men have created their own covenants with
rape and violence, only God's covenants stand.

The works of his hands are faithful and just; all
his precepts are trustworthy. They are established
for ever and ever, enacted in faithfulness and
uprightness.

—Psalm 111:7–8

The bride is purified and redeemed by the blood of Yeshua, and the sexually immoral are punished.

> It is God's will that you should be sanctified: that you should avoid sexual immorality; that each of you should learn to control your own body in a way that is holy and honorable, not in passionate lust like the pagans, who do not know God; and that in this matter no one should wrong or take advantage of a brother or sister. The Lord will punish all those who commit such sins, as we told you and warned you before.
>
> —1 THESSALONIANS 4:3–6

Giving in to evil desires such as rape makes a person a pagan who does not know God. Compromise and tolerance, using select scriptures of wrongful behaviors, places the offending men among the pagans, false religions, and Islam. However, God has made a plan to create good from all the evil that men do by the women becoming warriors.

> How long will you gad about, O you backsliding daughter? For the LORD has created a new thing in the earth—A woman shall encompass a man.
>
> —JEREMIAH 31:22, NKJV

The Hebrew says that women will encircle warring men, as though they are protecting the army. The question to the daughters, "How long will you gad about [hesitate]," shows that there is an initial hesitation to come to God. Part of the reason women hesitate is because so many man-made covenants have been made and are confused with God's Word. Women are sometimes uncertain about becoming a bride to Yeshua because the way men have treated their brides makes women question whether they will again be subjected to spousal rape and abuse. However, God is doing something new.

Another example of warring women is found in Psalms:

> *Adonai* [The Lord] gives the command; the women with the good news are a mighty army.
>
> —PSALM 68:11, CJB

Certain translations of Psalm 68:11 use the generic term "company," but the Hebrew clearly yields a feminine term for a warring population. Women become a mighty army at the command of God when they have the good news.

> Get up! Start threshing, daughter of Tziyon! "For I will make your horns like iron and your hoofs like bronze." You will crush many peoples and devote their plunder to ADONAI [the LORD], their wealth to the Lord of all the earth.
>
> —MICAH 4:13, CJB

A horn represents authority.

God will give the daughters of Zion authority. Their fathers may have denied them an inheritance; however, God is going to give them authority directly. The women will be devoting plunder to God. Plunder only comes from war, so God will be sending the daughters of Zion to war, and she will be victorious against many people. Rape is a way for men to try to force their way into a covenant, but through God and His Son, Yeshua, women are redeemed from defilement and will be given the strength to stand against their attackers in confirming God's holy covenant.

A NEW THING

*W*HEN YESHUA RETURNS, He will be coming back for a bride without spot or wrinkle. She is to be beautifully dressed with fine linen garments of pure white and adorned with jewels. The bride is all those who profess His name, yet the body of believers is composed of people with many blemishes and clothes stained with iniquity. The bride has been sullied because many lack understanding of what it means to be a bride. This misunderstanding may derive from the fact that the term "bride" is feminine.

Within the body of believers, women have been treated with contempt, dishonor, and scorn. As a result, becoming a bride is seen as a place of shame; either as a woman who is mistreated in marriage, or as a man who would not want to be a bride based on his low view of women.

The interaction men have with their brides correlates to how *the bride*—the body of believers—interacts with Yeshua. The body of believers stands in a weakened state because of the way women are treated. To come out of oppression, the body of believers must understand three things. First, women are not under a divine curse. Next, we must know the methods of physical, psychological, and spiritual warfare oppressors use and how to overcome them. Lastly, we must realize that women are redeemed by Messiah, and that God intends to do something new on the earth.

The idea of a divine curse originated with Adam's lie. With this lie Adam managed to convince Eve that death entered the world because she did not answer to him. However, the great fallacy of this lie is the circular logic of this argument. If she needed to answer to him, then he would be ultimately responsible for her actions because he did not try to stop her from eating the forbidden fruit. Then, Eve's desire for her husband and his ability to rule over her were used as evidence to support the lie. But the condition of Eve's servitude to Adam only came as a fruit of the sin after the event had taken place, meaning service to him was not implied during the time before sin. Yet Adam's lie was able to prevail because if Eve argued against the lie, this would only be used as more evidence to prove his point that women create strife and disharmony in what would have been paradise.

Eve was so battered down that she forgot her identity. Her purpose from the Hebrew meaning of the word נגד (*negad*)—which is typically translated "helper"—was to contend, strongly oppose, or support. The implementation of Adam's lie would only focus upon the support and "help" while ignoring the opposing nature of the woman, so that Adam would not have to be responsible for his shortcomings. Then, for the woman to act in opposition to the man, he would further blame her for sin, and use subjugation tactics to oppress this side of her nature to keep her from holding him accountable.

Genesis 3:16, which says that the woman's desire will be after her husband and he will rule over her, is a curse. However, Yeshua the Messiah came to break curses. Yet religious theology still relies on Adam's lie to perpetuate a curse that has been broken. The religious apply concepts like love to desire to make it seem as though Yeshua makes a woman desiring her husband to be a good thing, since Yeshua makes the reference to His return being like a Bridegroom coming for a bride. However, desire cannot be mistaken for love. Although the two words may have the same connotation, they are completely different.

Desire is a want, whereas love is wholeness. For a woman to desire is to long and yearn for something that will control her actions. Love, on the other hand, embraces her strengths and moves her in a way that empowers her identity. The redemption of Yeshua does not make desiring a man pleasant, but gives the woman love, which sets her free from desire. In a state of desire, a woman will tolerate a malevolent man in order to obtain what she desires. Tolerance is knowing something is wrong and merely accepting it. If a woman is being mistreated by a man while giving him silent submission, it is not love, it is tolerance.

The Scripture commands us to "Love the LORD your God" and to "Love your neighbor" (Deut. 6:5), not to tolerate. Love has a dual nature of passion and rebuke. Feelings of wholeness and completion are felt in the embrace of a lover, and this passion works together with rebuke to correct problems and empower the other party to continue to love. This fulfills the nature of the woman to support and help as well as to contend and oppose. Religious theology teaches that a woman who rebukes a man is out of place, which is precisely the opposite of the created nature of the woman.

The biggest stronghold that is presented to a woman would be if she chose to follow God and the husband remained satisfied in an ungodly lifestyle. The husband could use the position of the head and authority to block her from God. If she rebelled against him then she would be deemed ungodly for dishonoring the head, but if she followed she would be condemned to whatever lifestyle the husband preferred to lead. Since religion teaches that she is only meant to help the man, her only response is to try to submit her way out of the situation with the hope that his not experiencing any negative consequences will somehow move her husband to change his behavior. But if the husband's goal is subjugation, then the wife's submissive behavior simply rewards him for negative behavior, which will only increase his behavior.

This no-win situation is not what God intended for women. The curse is broken so that the woman does not have to be trapped by the desire for a husband. However, there is still the problem of men physically terrorizing women. This prophecy from Jeremiah is the resolution to that issue:

How long will you hesitate, you unruly daughter?
For ADONAI [the LORD] has created something new
on earth: a woman with the strengths of a man.
— JEREMIAH 31:21–22, CJB

The reference to the daughters as being unruly can be a wordplay on the undue assignment of the label "rebellious" to a woman who will not follow an ungodly man. It also refers to actual rebellion in the form of sin.

The question of "how long" shows the way women have shrunk back and been battered down as though they are unsure of what will happen when they approach God, especially if the Messiah presents Himself as a husband. Then the question is answered with reassurance that she will not continue to exist in the same battered state of subjugation and tyranny: "For the LORD has created something new on earth, a woman with the strengths of a man" (v. 22, CJB).

In the King James Version of the Bible, the word used in the scripture is "compass":

How long wilt thou go about, O thou backsliding
daughter? for the LORD hath created a new thing
in the earth, A woman shall compass a man.
— JEREMIAH 31:22, KJV

To compass means to go around. Although someone may cite how the man is the head, when God does a new thing, the woman can go around the man to receive directly from Yeshua—so then she will not be subject to a husband who blocks her from God.

When people typically talk about the hierarchy of God the Father, Yeshua the Messiah, the husband and the wife, they view it as a pyramid where the wife is the bottom layer. The pyramid is a symbol from Egypt and represents aspects of Egyptian religion and slavery. A more accurate symbol would be a circuit.

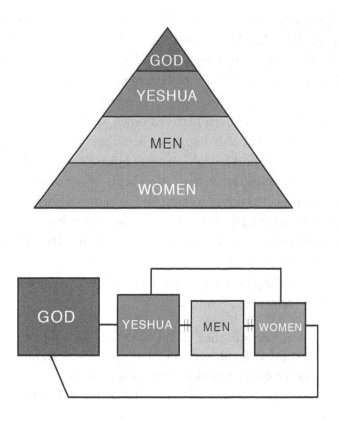

Once someone spoke of a dream they had about this hierarchy, where the relationship from God, Yeshua, and the husband and the wife was represented as a series circuit. God was the power source, and wires connected from left to right to Yeshua, then to the husband, then the wife. In the dream, though, the wife was able to circle around and reconnect directly back into the power source.

If the relationship between God, Yeshua, the husband, and the wife is viewed as a circuit as opposed to a pagan Egyptian pyramid, the husband does not have the power to cut his wife off or trample over her. In a series circuit, when one light is cut off, all the lights go out. This ties back into the way the prayers of a husband who does not honor his wife are hindered. Then, the wife's ability to go around the husband and complete the circuit is a reference to the prophecy where a woman will compass a man.

Other translations of Jeremiah 31:21–22 use the terms "encircle" or "surround." The definition of the term "surround" is more aggressive: "To enclose on all or nearly all sides; enclose; encompass, to cut off (a military unit, etc.) from communication or retreat by encircling." The military use of the definition is confirmed in the Hebrew. The word גבר (*gavar*), "mighty," used as the direct object of the statement, is a military term. The word סובב (*soavev*), which is translated as either "encircle," "compass," or "surround," is the same term used to describe the way the Israelites encompassed Jericho during their military defeat of the city.

When someone is encircled on all sides, it is checkmate! This prophecy is indicative of the women returning to her original identity to contend against the man. She will surround him on all sides, physically, emotionally, and spiritually, to put an end to his ungodly behavior and oppression. He will no longer be able to use the irrational "Adam theory," which is to blame the woman for sin coming into the world. He will not physically dominate her, or spiritually block her from union with her Messiah, Yeshua, or God.

Because of deception, the woman fell from her military might, but when God does a new thing, He will restore her to a position of authority. Most teachings meant to empower women stop at redemption. Women are taught to move past former abuse and mistreatment to embrace being a princess and loved by the Messiah and God. But like the woman, love has a dual nature. For a woman, experiencing the redemption of the Messiah is also about experiencing victory in war. This victory is not simply spiritual, through prayer and inner strength, but the glorious honor of winning a physical battle in God's army. Yeshua is returning for a bride who will rule and reign with Him—not under Him—as a warrior.

NOTES

Chapter 5: Covenant of Rape

1. During a military briefing about traveling to Turkey, my father, Master Sergeant Harvie Andrews Jr., was told of an incident where a man had looked at a woman for more than five seconds and was then pressed to marry her. The military had to expedite this man out of the country because of the conflict looking at that woman had created. So the men who were going on overseas tours of the Middle East were warned of this type of cultural belief.

2. Wikipedia.org, s.v. "Death by boiling," accessed September 30, 2015, https://en.wikipedia.org/wiki/Death_by _boiling#CITEREFChisholm1911.

3. Wikipedia.org, s.v. "Puerto Rican Day Parade attacks," accessed September 30, 2015, https://en.wikipedia.org/wiki/ Puerto_Rican_Day_Parade_attacks. See also "The Appeal #5," YouTube video, 8:36, posted by "PR Day Parade Sex Attacks DVD," October 1, 2009, https://www.youtube.com/watch?v=SYK jQohCuJ8; "Disturbing: Controversial Documentary Just Released About the Puerto Rican Day Parade s3x Attacks from 2000! 'Stop Grabbing Her,'" World Star Hip Hop.com, September 27, 2009, accessed September 30, 2015, http://www.worldstar hiphop.com/videos/video.php?v=wshhzm2R35Fciu9b28kE.

4. "UN Official Calls DR Congo 'Rape Capital of the World,'" BBC News, April 28, 2010, http://news.bbc.co.uk/2 /hi/8650112.stm. See also Wikipedia.org, s.v. "Sexual violence in the Democratic Republic of the Congo," accessed September 30, 2015, https://en.wikipedia.org/wiki/Sexual_violence_in_the _Democratic_Republic_of_the_Congo.

ABOUT THE AUTHOR

JASMINE DEANNE ANDREWS is a believer in Yeshua (Jesus) and she has a very romantic disposition. She envisions Yeshua as a gallant warrior returning for His bride. Her Bible studies have led her to investigate why marriages fail to meet brides' expectations and to develop teachings necessary to restore women's hopes and dreams about matrimony.

CONTACT THE AUTHOR

jasminedeanneandrews@gmail.com